Positive and Trusting Relationships with Children in Early Years Settings

ACHIEVING
EYPS

Positive and Trusting Relationships with Children in Early Years Settings

JESSICA JOHNSON

Series editors: Lyn Trodd and Gill Goodliff

LearningMatters

First published in 2010 by Learning Matters Ltd

British Library Cataloguing in Publication Data
A CIP record for this book is available from the British Library.

ISBN: 978 1 84445 402 0

This book is also available in the following ebook formats:

Adobe ebook ISBN: 978 1 84445 711 3
EPUB ebook ISBN: 978 1 84445 710 6
Kindle ISBN: 978 1 84445 996 4

Text design by Code 5 Design Associates Ltd
Cover design by Phil Barker
Project management by Swales & Willis Ltd, Exeter, Devon
Typeset by Swales & Willis Ltd, Exeter, Devon
Printed and bound in Great Britain by TJ International Ltd, Padstow, Cornwall

Learning Matters Ltd
33 Southernhay East
Exeter EX1 1NX
Tel: 01392 215560
info@learningmatters.co.uk
www.learningmatters.co.uk

FSC
Mixed Sources
Product group from well-managed
forests and other controlled sources

Cert no. SGS-COC-2482
www.fsc.org
© 1996 Forest Stewardship Council

Contents

Foreword from the series editors   vi

Acknowledgements   vii

About the author and the series editors   ix

1   Why trust? The key to positive relationships   1

2   Time to tune-in . . . and out   11

3   Respect for self and others   26

4   Understanding relationships with children in the context of professional boundaries   50

5   Trusting relationships as a secure foundation for children's learning   70

6   Supporting other Early Years practitioners to build positive relationships   94

7   Reflection and learning as an Early Years Professional   111

References   125

Index   132

Foreword from the series editors

This book is one of a series which will be of interest to all those following pathways towards achieving Early Years Professional Status (EYPS). This includes students on Sector-Endorsed Foundation Degree in Early Years programmes and undergraduate Early Childhood Studies degree courses as these awards are key routes towards EYPS.

The graduate EYP role was created as a key strategy in government commitment to improve the quality of Early Years care and education in England, especially in the private, voluntary and independent sectors. Policy documents and legislation such as *Every Child Matters: Change for Children,* DfES (2003); the *Ten Year Childcare Strategy: Choice for Parents – the Best Start for Children*, HMT (2004); and the Childcare Act (2006) identified the need for high-quality, well-trained and educated professionals to work with the youngest children. The government's aim – restated in the 2020 Children and Young People's Workforce Strategy (DCSF, 2008) – is to have a graduate-led children's workforce with an Early Years Professional (EYP) in Children's Centres by 2010 and in every full day care setting by 2015, with two graduates in disadvantaged areas.

This book is distinctive in the series in that its particular focus is on the interpersonal understanding and skills of the EYP in order to work within the Early Years Foundation Stage in promoting 'Positive Relationships'. It recognises the importance of emotional literacy as an aspect of professionalism and as fundamental to a commitment to young children's well-being and development.

As a leader of practice, excellent interpersonal skills are vital if the EYP is to model high-quality practice to colleagues and to be successful in influencing other practitioners and helping them reflect on and improve the way they work with children, families and colleagues. Jessica Johnson's approach is to look at how EYPs can build and sustain trust in relationships between the EYP and children and other adults. Each chapter considers the responsibilities of an EYP for promoting positive relationships and explores the skills needed to fulfil them. Jessica uses case studies and self-assessment questions to focus the attention of the reader on how to meet the EYP Standards in full, the expectations of excellent practice of an EYP and also to reflect critically on the issues they raise.

June 2010

Lyn Trodd and Gill Goodliff

Acknowledgements

Positive and trusting relationships throughout my life have enabled me to risk 'having-a-go' at writing this book. Thanks are due, specifically, to the following individuals.

My parents – Dorothy and Fred Chinnick – provided consistent unconditional love, so have to come first. This is underpinned by a firm, trusting relationship with God, as a Christian. My mother, as a trained 'nanny', shared the same zest for life with her 'charges' as with her own children, showing consistency between personal and professional relationship skills. Pauleen Preston (1930-2010), valued the attachment to her 'Nanny' throughout life, with a real sense of 'fun', curiosity, and the ability to share 'stories'.

The ever-growing Early Years Team at Kingston University keep the realities of maintaining positive and trusting relationships at work alive through busy times as 'I' becomes 'we'! We are grateful to Anne Rawlings for challenging us to keep ahead of change in Early Years and Inter-professional Practice and to Daryl Maisey for inspirational leadership through those changes! My thanks are to all the lecturing and administration team, with Head of School of Education, Andy Hudson, for creating an example of a dynamic environment, encapsulating the need for collaborative working skills as we retain positive learning dispositions!

I have been privileged to work with Neil Blumsom (Kingston), Sue Thompson (Merton), and Alison Archibald and Claire Grayson (Richmond) to develop the Kingston, Merton and Richmond Early Years Professional Support Network. We are on a continuous learning journey together and I am grateful to all who have provided material for this book. I only wish we had more time to do justice to the changes happening within early years practice – it is hard to keep up! Special thanks are due to contributors Bex Halden and Geraldine Hill for inspirational input to Network meetings. Written excerpts in this book can never fully capture the true engagement of live presentations. Likewise representation of the babies, young children, families and colleagues only touches on the impact of 'tuning-in' – thanks to all.

Thanks are also due to Jane Mitchell, a past Foundation Degree, BA (Hons) Early Years student who keeps us up-to-date writing relevant articles! Along with past and present students on these expanding courses, and staff across nine colleges, you keep me convinced that we have a quest to develop positive, trusting relationships through conflict and change . . . remembering to celebrate achievements! We certainly show resilience!

Acknowledgements

Lyn Trodd has been the driving force behind having this key topic within the Early Years Professional Status series. I have felt supported throughout this opportunity and am grateful for her patient company in my own learning journey. Jennifer Clark, the development editor, has guided me through this 'new world' and kept me on track – many thanks.

Final thanks are due to my immediate family – Wes, Stephen, Rachael and Liz – who provide love and support, and the many others who patiently encourage me from a distance. I look forward to spending real time with you all again!

June 2010

Jessica Johnson

About the author and the series editors

Jessica Johnson

Jessica Johnson is Senior Lecturer in Early Years at Kingston University and currently Programme Leader for the Sector-Endorsed Foundation Degree in Early Years, Course Leader for the BA (Hons) 'top-up' in Early Years Education and Care, EYPS Senior Assessor and Project Leader for the Kingston, Merton and Richmond EYP Support Network. Rite of passage to this role started in the National Health Service, tuning-in to babies, young children and their families at The Hospital for Sick Children, Great Ormond Street. They initiated ongoing curiosity in child development – specifically social and emotional relationships. Chameleon-like, she has experienced first-hand the challenges in creating positive, trusting relationships through roles in health, social care, education and as a mediator in the voluntary sector.

Lyn Trodd

Lyn Trodd is Head of Children's Workforce Development at the University of Hertfordshire. Lyn is the Chair of the National Network of Sector-Endorsed Foundation Degrees in Early Years. She was involved in the design of Early Years Professional Status and helped to pilot the Validation Pathway when it first became available. Lyn has published and edited a range of articles, national and international conference papers and books focusing on self-efficacy in the child and the practitioner and also the professional identity and role of adults who work with young children.

Gill Goodliff

Gill Goodliff is a Senior Lecturer and Head of Awards for Early Years at the Open University where she has developed and chaired courses on the Sector-Endorsed Foundation Degree and as a Lead Assessor for Early Years Professional Status. Her professional work with young children and their families was predominantly in the voluntary sector. Her research interests centre on the professional identities of early years practitioners and young children's spirituality.

1 Why trust? The key to positive relationships

Each generation begins anew with fresh, eager trusting faces of babies, ready to love and create a new world.

L. De Mause (2002) cited in The Next Generation report
(The Centre for Social Justice, 2008)

CHAPTER OBJECTIVES

This chapter provides a rationale for *Positive and Trusting Relationships with Children in Early Years Settings*.

Definitions of key terms, including trust and positive relationships, provide an underpinning for the more detailed, specific explorations in further chapters.

Links between current research and daily Early Years practice acknowledge the growing awareness of the impact of these relationships on the physical, emotional, social and intellectual development of the young child.

Reflective and practical tasks, case studies and self-assessment activities are included to help Early Years practitioners identify these links, with reference to the Early Years Foundation Stage (EYFS) and the following Standards for Early Years Professional Status (EYPS):

S18: Promote children's rights, equality, inclusion and anti-discriminatory practice in all aspects of their practice.

S25: Establish fair, respectful, trusting, supportive and constructive relationships with children.

S26: Communicate sensitively and effectively with children from birth to the end of the Foundation Stage.

S27: Listen to children, pay attention to what they say and value and respect their views.

S28: Demonstrate the positive values, attitudes and behaviour they expect from children.

After reading this chapter you should be able to:

- reflect on levels of trust within past and present experiences of relationships with children, parents and colleagues;
- appraise critically some of the strategies used within Early Years practice to establish relationships with babies and young children;
- begin to apply models of relationship behaviour as you prepare to meet the Standards for EYPS.

Introduction

Do the babies and young children we meet with every day come with *fresh, eager trusting faces*? Do we sense they are *ready to love*? Are we, as Early Years Professionals (EYPs), consciously able to respond with trust and love, encouraging their curiosity, allowing them to take risks and building up their resilience, which is essential if they are to *create a new world*? We know babies at birth are totally dependent on adults to survive but how can we create positive relationships with young children and extend this innate, calculated trust as they grow and develop?

This book will explore these questions, along with others, that acknowledge the vital, yet challenging, role Early Years practitioners play as babies and young children establish, maintain and develop their trust in others, building up trust in themselves in the process. The focus, initially, will be the baby and child, trying to identify what they need, seek and bring to relationships with adult carers and other children. The adult chooses, whether consciously or not, ways to both receive the communications, interpret and understand the message and respond, creating active dialogue. Competent Early Years practitioners tune-in to the needs of the individuals – babies, children and adults. Chapter 2 will acknowledge why this 'tuning-in' is crucial to the brain development of babies and young children, acknowledging the power of these early relationships on the long-term social and emotional development of children. This, in turn, enables children to make the most of cognitive learning opportunities – opening up a holistic approach to child development within these secondary relationships (Chapter 5). Tuning-in to the primary attachment figures – parents/carers – also requires astute observation and active listening skills, often hard when time together is at a premium. There is scope within Chapter 4 to see if the term 'trust' can describe practitioner/child relationships in a way that safely encompasses love and care, acknowledging professional boundaries.

The key EYPS Standard S25: *Establish fair, respectful, trusting, supportive and constructive relationships with children* requires evidence from an EYP of their ability to **create** and **build up** positive relationships, with trust as a central attribute. Here, the responsibility appears to move to the EYP to start and maintain the relationship within their setting.

The case studies and reflective and practical tasks throughout this book will provide opportunities to explore these interplays between child and adult, both having an effect on the establishment of the constructive relationships. Each of the descriptive terms – *fair, respectful, supportive* and *constructive* – will be considered throughout, with trust identified as underpinning them all. The umbrella term often used is 'positive relationships' but the supportive and constructive elements required within Standard 25 acknowledge that *neutral and negative relationships* may also exist. An EYP, as a skilful, co-operative communicator, may be able to lead and support other practitioners in recognising early signs of these and try to instigate change (Chapter 6). This book seeks to go under the 'positive relationships' umbrella and value what often seem to be commonplace interactions, linking them to current research and theories. The hope is that EYPs will be empowered to confidently select from a variety of communication strategies, building on whatever level of trust babies and children come with from relationships with their primary carers.

REFLECTIVE TASK

Learning from a baby or child

It is the babies and young children who, when we found ways to listen carefully enough, taught us most about what matters in nurseries, often long before they could talk.

(Elfer et al., 2009, page v)

Think back to an experience where you learnt from a baby or child.

- *What were you trying to do at the time e.g. feed them, play, clear up?*
- *What did they do or say that had an impact on you?*
- *What did you learn from this, and did it bring about any change – short or long term?*
- *Can this experience be seen, like those in the above quote, to say anything about what mattered to your baby or child?*
- *What skills did you require to enable you to learn from them?*

An EYP requires the energy, commitment, knowledge and expertise to match and encourage the motivation of expectant children in the setting. EYPs can act as role models to their colleagues. An exploration of ways to build trust within positive relationships will now follow.

What is 'trust'?

Trust and relationships take time to form: you cannot do them in a fast food way.

(Seldon, 2009a, page 2)

Trust is defined in the *Penguin English Dictionary* (1992) as *confident belief in or reliance on the ability, character, honesty of somebody or something.* We may trust the chair we are sitting on to stay firm and not let us down. We have learnt this through a mixture of knowledge about what a chair is, observation of others using a chair and our own personal experience – for better or for worse! For most of the time we trust chairs to carry out their role, only likely to be consciously aware when they are not doing what we expect – collapsing or being uncomfortable!

The content of this book will explore how babies and young children gain *confident belief or reliance on the ability, character and honesty* of their Early Years practitioners/Key Person. Starting with 'tuning-in' to the needs of the individual baby or child, the developing relationship will have to be nurtured until finally bringing about closure. Throughout, the young child should be protected in order to *do or be without fear or misgiving* – also within the definition of trust. These supportive and constructive practitioner skills within professional boundaries should allow for risk-taking and the building up of resilience, to be covered in Chapter 4. The practitioner must seek to be *trustworthy: dependable, reliable* (the *Penguin English Dictionary*, 1992).

However, *it takes years to build up trust and only seconds to destroy it* (anon).

Babies and young children may well be meeting with a number of different carers. One of the attributes of an EYP is to *lead and support others* (CWDC, 2008, page 5). As *catalysts for change* they are in a prime position to help other practitioners understand the impact on relationship building of daily interactions with under 5s. This becomes a *relationship-based approach* to Early Years practice.

What are positive relationships?

Positive relationships tend to be portrayed in terms of interactive behaviour e.g. *'J. smiled back at 6 month old C., mirroring her happy expression'*. These seemingly small responses impact on brain development, with the creation of new neural pathways (Trevarthen, 2009). Evidence from neurological research shows how these 'mirror moments' lead to implications for physical, social, emotional and cognitive achievement.

The second principle of the EYFS states:

> *Positive Relationships – children learn to be strong and independent from a base of loving and secure relationships with parents and/or a Key Person.*

> (Department for Children, Schools and Families (DCSF), 2008a, page 5)

The child is the learner here, the adults the providers of a loving, secure relationship base. There are implications for both parties that will be covered in more detail in Chapter 2. The child has already been recognised as 'Unique' in the first principle of the EYFS (DCSF, 2008a). This uniqueness values each child as *a competent learner from birth who can be resilient, capable, confident and self-assured.* Again, these are powerful terms that require ownership by those caring for all young children. The *'can be'* requires an expectancy on behalf of the EYP to provide both opportunities which will enable the child to develop strategies to be resilient and activities to show to themselves and others that they are capable. These will lead to increased confidence and self-assurance. Effort is coming from all parties.

To enable this learning and development to occur Early Years practitioners are expected to:

- *form warm, caring relationships with children in the group;*
- *establish constructive relationships with parents, with everyone in the setting and with workers from other agencies;*
- *find opportunities to give encouragement to children, with practitioners acting as role models who value differences and take account of different needs and expectations;*
- *plan for opportunities for children to play and learn, sometimes alone and sometimes in groups of varying sizes.*

> (DCSF, 2008a, page 24)

Similar suggestions are made against each of the other five areas within the EYFS, and they will be addressed at later stages in this book. Here, warm, caring, relationships with children are directly linked with constructive relationships between practitioners and parents, colleagues and other professionals. It is the combination of these which often create the sense of well-being and emotional security experienced by parents when they visit a setting prior to their young child starting. Chapter 2 will look at the key communication skills required to attain this open, welcoming aura, but in order to fully appreciate and value the impact of these relationships it is important for practitioners to know what is happening to themselves as well as the developing child.

The Early Years Professional as a key for establishing positive relationships

To sustain warm, caring relationships with all children is often more challenging than the cosy picture implied. What is really required is an environment that allows for growth/learning for both child and adult, what Carl Rogers termed a *growth-promoting climate* (Rogers, 1995, page 115). He states the following three conditions are required in *any* relationship where the development of the individual is the goal.

1. 'Genuineness', realness or congruence – the person (Early Years practitioner) is himself or herself in the relationship.

2. 'Unconditional positive regard' – acceptance or caring for a baby, child or adult regardless of what is happening.

3. 'Empathic understanding' – the ability to sense accurately what the baby, child or adult is feeling.

PRACTICAL TASK

Consider an adult or child that you trust

- *Take each of Carl Rogers' three conditions in turn.*

- *See if you can identify any examples of behaviour shown by your trusted person.*

- *Then see if you can identify ways you show these behaviours to them.*

'Growth-promoting climate' – 3 conditions (Rogers)	Examples of behaviour *from* your trusted person	Examples of your behaviour *to* your trusted person
Genuineness, realness or congruence	Ways in which the person is 'themself':	Ways in which you are able to be yourself in their presence:
Unconditional positive regard	Ways in which they accept or care for you regardless of what is happening:	Ways in which you can accept and care for them regardless of what is happening:
Empathic understanding	Ways in which they sense accurately what you are feeling:	Ways in which you sense accurately what they are feeling:

- *Compare the columns. Are they evenly balanced? There is no right or wrong here, just a way of exploring what is happening within a relationship.*

- *Compare the rows. Do you have evidence in all or are some empty? Again, there is no right or wrong here, just a way of exploring what is happening.*

Each brings its own demands on the individual and may only be possible, at times, when there is respect for oneself as well as for the other. Chapter 3 will look critically at how realistic it is for Early Years practitioners to develop these abilities and what the impact may be on the learning and development of the babies and children in their settings.

Although the focus in this book is on relationships with children in Early Years settings, any practitioner is aware of how these relationships energise but also drain them. In the same way that those who care for others need to care for themselves and be prepared to receive care from others, those who seek to develop positive relationships with others benefit from a positive awareness of themselves and of being able to receive within other positive relationships. Each individual can find their own way to re-energise, but it is worth looking at behaviour demonstrated within a trusting relationship, using Rogers' conditions.

Levels of relationship: attachment and the Key Person

Babies and young children in Early Years settings are making crucial secondary attachments with staff, building on those with their primary carers. Professional boundaries need to be clarified for maintenance of secure, healthy relationships and later chapters will draw on developments from John Bowlby's attachment theory (1999), using case studies and reflective tasks.

As 'key persons' (Elfer *et al.*, 2009) role-model positive relationships within 'secondary attachments' babies and children are provided with opportunities to experience trusting

---

REFLECTIVE TASK

Opportunities for experiencing trust and mistrust
Think of examples within the normal routines of a baby's/toddler's/young child's day where:

- *trust can be built up;*
- *mistrust experienced.*

Erikson's eight stages of life-span development (1950) arose from personal observation within communities. He saw the first stage being one of constructive tension, primarily from birth to eighteen months, between trust and mistrust.

What the child acquires at a given stage is a certain **ratio** between the positive and negative, which if the balance is toward the positive, will help him to meet later crises with a better chance for unimpaired total development.

(Erikson, 1968)

These early stages continue to be represented throughout life.

Reflect on your own examples in relation to Erikson's theory. Are there any changes you may make to your practice that will recognise and value both trust and mistrust?

relationships. Through these, they will start to create their own strategies and boundary-setting for further relationships. EYPs can be instrumental in providing these opportunities, highlighted by examples in Chapters 2, 3, 4 and 5.

Trust and the national picture

The Every Child Matters (ECM) agenda, arising from the Green Paper (Department for Education and Skills (DfES), 2003), is supposedly embedded within all elements of practice for the children's workforce. So, to what extent are aspects of positive relationships included within the original 2003 framework? Below are some selected aims within each of the five outcomes of ECM. Identify which ones are considered when creating long-term plans in your setting.

Table 1.1 The five outcomes of Every Child Matters

Be healthy	Stay safe	Enjoy and achieve	Make a positive contribution	Achieve economic well-being
Aims include:	Aims include:	Aims include:	Aims include:	Aims include:
Mentally and emotionally healthy.	Have security, stability and are cared for;	Ready for school;	Engage in decision-making;	Live in decent homes and sustainable communities;
	Safe from maltreatment, neglect, violence and sexual exploitation;	Achieve personal and social development and enjoy recreation.	Support the community and the environment;	
			Engage in law-abiding and positive behaviour;	Live in households free from low income.
	Safe from bullying and discrimination.		Develop positive behaviour and choose not to bully or discriminate;	
			Develop self-confidence and successfully deal with significant life changes and challenges.	

www.dcsf.gov.uk/childrensplan/downloads/ECM%20outcomes%20framework.pdf (accessed 24 May 2010)

Links to EYP S05: The current legal requirements, national policies and guidance on health and safety, safeguarding and promoting the well-being of children and their implications for Early Years settings.

The Common Core of Skills and Knowledge (DfES, 2005) has sought to identify the key skills and knowledge required to meet the ECM outcomes by all practitioners within the children's workforce, including Early Years practitioners. Seen as a priority are skills and knowledge to effectively communicate and engage with children, young people and their families.

*A key part of effective communication and engagement is **trust** between the workforce, children, young people and their carers; and between and within different sectors of the workforce itself.*

This 'first' skill involves listening and building empathy, starting with the need to build on the primary attachments.

- Establish rapport and respectful, **trusting** relationships with children, young people, their families and carers.

CASE STUDY

Childcare at 6 months

Alison and Paul are thinking carefully about childcare for 6-month-old Toby, talking to friends, relatives, health visitor and Family Information Services about the range of local provision. Alison had several miscarriages so they were thrilled by Toby's safe arrival. He was breast-fed for four weeks but is now fully bottle-fed. Toby continually surprises them with his achievements, the latest being able to sit for a few moments unsupported before toppling sideways.

Both are full-time employed, with Alison due to return from maternity leave.

The childcare options, so far, are as follows:

- *one independent day nursery, up to five days a week;*

- *one nursery within a Children's Centre, vacancy for three days a week;*

- *Paul's mother – a car-drive away – maximum two days a week;*

- *working at home one day a week;*

- *childminder in the same road, but no vacancies at present.*

REFLECTIVE TASK

Research consistently shows that a healthy ego and emotional security are essential to learning, and it's the relationships with parents and caregivers — particularly in the first year of life — that foster trust, autonomy, and initiative as the child matures. Children who have trusting, highly interactive relationships with their parents and caregivers display more active curiosity and initiate more learning opportunities.

(Espinosa, 2009)

Use your knowledge and skills in relation to establishing and maintaining positive and trusting relationships with parents and babies. Identify three strategies you may offer to Alison and Paul if they approach you about Toby starting at your setting.

Relationships for Early Years Professionals

'Relationships with Children' is one of the six groups of Early Years Professional Standards (CWDC, 2008, pages 45–52) highlighting *the significance of building and maintaining personal relationships in supporting the well-being, learning and development of babies, toddlers and young children.*

An EYP is expected to demonstrate S25: *Establish fair, respectful, trusting, supportive and constructive relationships with children* within their own personal practice and through leading and supporting others. The following chapters in this book will identify ways to do both, adapting McMullen and Dixon's model for a *relationship-based approach* (2009). This sees trusting relationships developing over a period of time through being alert to three different types of practice – all of which are relevant to Early Years settings – 'mindful', 'respectful' and 'reflective'.

- **'Mindful'** recognises the need for EYPs to be 'in the moment' – alert and aware of the needs of the babies and young children (Chapters 2 and 4).

- **'Respectful'** requires recognition of differing values and beliefs, seeking to understand differing points of view in order to reach a fair consensus that is best for all parties (Chapters 3 and 5).

- **'Reflective'** acknowledges the EYP's ability to see the reflective practitioner cycle of planning, implementation and evaluation/reflection as a key process for developing relationships. This is specifically relevant when it comes to leading and supporting others (Chapters 6 and 7).

Relationships are likely to be enriched when these three types of practice are able to complement each other. Levels of trust and the depth of positive relationships may be hard to measure and evaluate, but consideration of daily interactions within this model will allow EYPs to identify potential areas for change and strategies to enhance their relationships with babies, children, families and colleagues.

C H A P T E R   S U M M A R Y

In this chapter trust has been identified as being central to the development of positive relationships in Early Years, alongside being *fair, respectful, supportive and constructive* (EYP Standard 25). The EYP is recognised as having skills and knowledge to provide optimum care and learning opportunities for 0–5 year olds, while also leading and supporting others to do likewise. This is an amazing relationship role, yet so often this element is seen as underpinning the more specific, and perhaps more easily measurable, care and education tasks. Early Years practitioners have a key role in helping the under 5s develop a realistic trust in others as well as themselves. This is enhanced by working in partnership with the primary carers who have, and are establishing, the initial attachments, as well as other secondary carers (EYP Standards 25–28).

Babies and young children have an innate, calculated trust that their carers will meet their basic needs. Current neurological research shows that the way these needs are responded to and met, or not, influences the development of neurological pathways within the brain. This, in turn, impacts on the ability to learn. Developing positive relationships with others demands time and energy. EYPs need to be alert to receive from others within relationships as well as give, finding trusting relationships that will energise themselves.

Positive relationships are central to the Common Core of Skills and Knowledge (DfES, 2005) required for all childcare workers in England at present as they address the five outcomes of the Every Child Matters agenda (2003).

Moving on

The following chapter will focus on initial interactions between babies and young children and Early Years practitioners. Skills and strategies that support this 'tuning-in . . . and out' will be critically analysed, linking with key theories of attachment and the impact on neurological development.

Self-assessment questions

1 What evidence do I currently have of myself as a role model of positive relationships with:

a) 0–20 month olds?

b) 16–36 month olds?

c) 30–60 month olds?

d) parents/primary carers?

2 Take one skill you have demonstrated within this evidence. Look for links with the different theories and models introduced in this chapter. Can you identify a preferred theory/model?

3 When comparing evidence across the four groups:

- which provides the strongest evidence of trusting relationships?

- which will benefit most from exploring additional strategies to develop trust within the relationships?

FURTHER READING

Duffy, A, Chambers, F, Croughan, S and Stephens, J (2006) Respecting Babies and Young Children, in *Working with Babies and Children Under Three*. Oxford: Heinemann.

Elfer, P, Goldschmeid, E and Selleck, D (2009) *Key Persons in the Nursery. Building Relationships for Quality Provision*. Oxford: David Fulton Publishers.

The Centre for Social Justice (2008) *The Next Generation. A Policy Report from the Early Years Commission*. London: The Centre for Social Justice.

2 Time to tune-in . . . and out

What makes the right person right is when the holding takes place in the context of a relationship of trust, reliability, familiarity and respect.

(Elfer *et al.* 2009, page 12)

This chapter explores the impact of brief, daily interactions on establishing positive and trusting relationships between Early Years practitioners and 0–5 year olds.

It sets the scene for material in later chapters, providing an introduction to the importance of secure secondary attachments while valuing primary attachments within a family. Evidence arising from developments in neuroscience is used to demonstrate how these initial communications set up new neural connections in the brain in preparation for ongoing learning and development.

Reflective and practical tasks and case studies will link to the following EYPS Standards:

S25: Establish fair, respectful, trusting, supportive and constructive relationships with children.

S26: Communicate sensitively and effectively with children from birth to the end of the Foundation Stage.

S27: Listen to children, pay attention to what they say and value and respect their views.

S29: Recognise and respect the influential and enduring contribution that families and parents/carers can make to children's development, well-being and learning.

S30: Establish fair, respectful, trusting and constructive relationships with families and parents/carers, and communicate sensitively and effectively with them.

S31: Work in partnership with families and parents/carers, at home and in the setting, to nurture children, to help them develop and to improve outcomes for them.

After reading this chapter you should be able to:

- identify opportunities within Early Years settings for 'tuning-in and out' to babies and young children;
- understand the impact these, sometimes brief, interactions have on brain development and ongoing social and emotional literacy;
- select communication skills and strategies to maximise opportunities for developing secure secondary attachments with positive, trusting relationships;
- reflect on sensitive, effective ways to nurture children, in partnership with parents and carers in primary attachments.

Introduction

The focus in this chapter is on the Early Years practitioner's responses to babies and young children as they seek to establish fair, respectful, trusting, supportive and constructive relationships. A range of verbal and non-verbal strategies to *make the right person right* in relation to *holding* a child in both the physical and psychological sense will be explored. Examples of 'attunement' between adults and children, children to children and adult to adult will be provided, linked to attachment and communication theories and their impact on creating neural (nerve) connections within a changing brain (neuroscience). These examples include:

- 'proto-conversations' between adults and babies;

- the power of 'No!';

- the wonder of 'How?' and 'Why?'.

Tuning-out' will explore the different ways to 'let be' and 'say goodbye' and the relevance of these to establishing positive, trusting relationships.

First impressions

Babies and young children actively seek close relationships with their parents and other primary caregivers (DCSF, 2008a, page 22). What are babies and young children looking for when they put effort into finding close relationships? As with all mammals, they are dependent on others to satisfy their basic needs, also rights, for care provision and protection (UNCRC, 1989).

However, as human beings, we are increasingly learning how the human brain grows and develops in direct response to social and emotional interactions. Infants have, intuitively, been stimulating their own brain development. Babies and young children are looking for people who 'cue in' to their communications and are willing to extend them. In these roles they become active participants within these relationships. Professional staff may need to catch up on recognising ways to fully acknowledge these participation rights (UNCRC, 1989) that occur as baby and child make their first encounters with practitioners in a setting. These new relationships will be seen as 'secondary attachments' (Bowlby, 2009).

PRACTICAL TASK

First meetings
Think about the **first** *time you met* **ONE** *baby or young child as they joined your setting. Write a description of this baby or child in one paragraph, just using narrative. Then analyse your description, highlighting recognition of any of the following:*

- *facial expression;*

- *body posture;*

- *touch;*

- *general appearance;*

- *specific vocabulary;*
- *non-specific vocabulary e.g. babbling, crying;*
- *movement;*
- *relationship to parent/carer;*
- *relationship to sibling;*
- *relationship to self;*
- *relationship to other staff and/or children;*
- *smell.*

What remains un-highlighted in your paragraph?

Rank your descriptors, with most commonly used at the top e.g.: general appearance; non-specific vocabulary; relationship with parent.

You may like to refer back to this later in the chapter.

While mainly focusing on looking and hearing as key senses for 'tuning-in', touch and smell also become a crucial communication link as babies and young children differentiate between their familial carers and Early Years practitioners; as one young boy commented as I sat close to him after a break, *'Mmm . . . coffee!'*. I had never thought of information being shared through breath smell before. It is important to remain alert for babies, young children and adults with limited hearing and vision who are likely to respond to an increased variety of sensory opportunities to 'tune-in'.

REFLECTIVE TASK

Fourteen-month-old Phillip came towards me, snuggled in on the left hip and arm of his tall father, with a small teddy in his right hand. As I greeted them, Phillip grabbed the small finger of my right hand with his left hand and pulled me closer. He held my gaze and started to talk rapidly.

'Bbb . . . mm . . . aa . . . car . . . bb . . . dd . . . car . . .' I replied, *'So you saw the car, Phillip?'*

'Car . . . mm . . . dada . . . ca. . . . ?' *'Phillip, was that Daddy and the car?'*

'Aaa . . . sky . . . bb . . . sky.' (Phillip looked up)

'You can see the sky too. What's there, Phillip?'

Phillip continues to look up, then drops Teddy. 'Shall I pick up Teddy?'

He looks down so I reach and pick up Teddy while he still clings onto my finger, only letting go when I hand him the bear. His conversation then returns to his father. As a medium for communication, holding my finger seemed as important to Phillip as

REFLECTIVE TASK *continued*

maintaining eye contact and having a verbal 'conversation'. This experience links closely to the following key points within the 'Development Matters' column for Making Relationships, Personal, Social and Emotional Development for 8–20 months (DCSF, 2008a, page 32):

- seek to gain attention in a variety of ways, drawing others into social interaction;

- use their developing physical skills to make social contact.

How was I showing Phillip that I was 'tuning-in'? What are the implications here for 'tuning-in . . . and out'?

A scientific study by Sieratzki and Woll (2005) confirms what many expert practitioners working with babies know about the emotional impact of touch. Touch is the *most basic and reciprocal mode of interactions, being more direct and immediate if an infant is held to the left side of the body* (Sieratzki and Woll, 2005, pages 613–14).

PRACTICAL TASK

Exploring smell and touch as 'tuning-in' strategies
In the table below:

- *provide examples of three types of touch and smell that may be evident when a practitioner meets and greets a baby or child;*

- *comment on their impact on communication;*

- *provide three recommendations you may make as a leader and supporter of Early Years practitioners, encouraging them to value sensory opportunities to 'tune-in'.*

Types of touch	Impact on communication	Types of smell	Impact on communication
Stroking baby's cheek with outside of finger	'Aaah!' Slowing down Calming	Cigarette 'breath'	May be familiar/'comfortable' if family smoke . . . or overpowering . . . 'turning away' 'uncomfortable'
Example 1		Example 1	
Example 2		Example 2	
Example 3		Example 3	
Three recommended 'tuning-in' strategies for 'touch'		Three recommended 'tuning-in' strategies for 'smell'	
1.		1.	
2.		2.	
3.		3.	

Looking for similarities

As new relationships are made between babies and young children and Early Years practitioners, Standard 29 for EYPS acts as a firm reminder of the need to *recognise and respect the influential and enduring contribution that families and parents/carers can make to children's development, well-being and learning.* Relationships with these primary attachment figures provide a 'norm' when exploring other relationships. Babies and young children are known to look for similarities even in facial construction. Schore (2009) has even recorded an unconscious preference for female faces in the first five months of life!

As babies take an interest in other babies and children, as well as adults, the smile becomes an opening introduction, often after comparatively lengthy intense observation. A returned smile is known to generate further attempts at communication, such as gurgling, babbling and physical movement, possibly reaching out to touch the 'other'. Johnson (2000) argues that babies' brains are pre-wired to connect up to facial images, then opening up neural pathways for further face recognition. Along with Morton (Johnson and Morton, 1991), he developed the CONSPEC – conspecific face recognition system – to show that *we are born with a conspecific face recognition system which is a brain system that passes on information about the structure of the human face to the brain cortex for further analysis, sufficient to direct the infant's gaze to another person's face for the purpose of comparison* (Doherty and Hughes, 2009, page 379). This supports the 'seeking out' of others for more than just satisfying provision and protection needs – active participation is needed to enter social and emotional interactions. Can we allow time for babies and young children to compare and contrast our appearance, with the understanding that at the same time as this is happening, changes may be occurring?

REFLECTIVE TASK

Face comparison: under the 'gaze'!

How do we respond when children make comments about our appearance or that of other adults or children? Neuroscience is telling us that as we see facial and body outlines co-ordinates are set up, like points on a map, in our brains. Norms become established from what we see, so the way we present ourselves to the babies and young children in our care helps to create their personal norms. In a non-judgemental way look around at the images you present (these may be reinforced by staff pictures in entrance halls!). How do we introduce new people to babies and young children, acknowledging that this will extend their 'norm'?

Brief, daily interactions – rhythms and routines

Gerhardt (2004, page 196) talks about the *best responsiveness for babies* being *the contingent kind*, when parent or caregiver responds *to the actual need of the particular baby not to their own idea of what the baby may need*. Often, to find out what those needs are throughout the day, all our senses come into play, as in the initial quote in this chapter *making the right person right*. Parents who demonstrate this ability with their baby/child can provide specific insight and expertise about their child for the Early Years practitioner.

Parents and immediate family members most easily understand their babies' and children's communications and can often interpret for others (DCSF, 2008a, page 41).

Settings may have a variety of strategies in place for parents to share specific knowledge about practical ways to feed, settle, nappy change, communicate with their child. These will be discussed in more detail in Chapter 3 in relation to respect of self and others. In relation to 'tuning-in . . . and out' though, observing the way the parent and child interact can provide an image of established communication skills. Home visits can also provide useful scenarios, as it is here the initial, personal dialogues have taken place, fine-tuning patterns in the young child's brain. There is likely to have been familiar patterning of rhythms and voice intonation, similar across cultures (Fogel, 1993–4; Trevarthen, 2004) where the adult and child co-regulate their communication. By watching the parent/child interaction, the EYP may be able to identify vocabulary and patterns that can also be used within the setting. There may also be times to extend the dialogue sensitively, but more extensive coverage of this will follow, too, in the next chapter, where we will look at how the practitioner may model communication to the parent.

Babies and young children have an ability for *social referencing* (Doherty and Hughes, 2009, page 346), where they look to the emotional response of a familiar person to something new, helping them to make sense of a different situation. Look back to your description of the new child in the practical task, page 12. Was 'social referencing' evident? An EYP can relate provision they make for this to S31: *Work in partnership with families and parents/carers, at home and in the setting, to nurture children, to help them develop and to improve outcomes for them.*

Initially, parent – mother mainly – and baby will have developed this means of 'tuning-in' to the emotions of each. The work of developmental scientist Colwyn Trevarthen (2004) has provided us with minutely detailed recordings of these sensitive interactions, noting rhythm, pitch, voice-tone and timing to fractions of a second of mother and baby communication. A mutual gaze is maintained throughout these intense, if brief, patterned periods:

- mother makes utterances;
- followed by a rest;
- the baby picks up with short, repetitive sounds with rhythmic intonation and undulating pitch;
- then turn-taking occurs;
- with an older baby, this lengthens with a sense of 'teasing' at times.

This has been likened to a rhythmic dance and has been found to be similar across cultures through further studies (Bateson, 1979; Karmiloff–Smith, 1994; Trevarthen, 1993, 2004). In this mother/baby interaction Trevarthen states the *quality of emotion is immediately affected by the feelings she expresses relative to what the baby does. The positiveness of contact is defined as matching strands of emotional reaction in the two of them. There is a sense of co-regulation – continuous unfolding of individual action modified by the continuously changing actions of the partner* (Doherty and Hughes, 2009, page 465).

PRACTICAL TASK

'Proto-conversations' between adults and babies

Can Early Years practitioners 'tune-in' as parents do, with the knowledge that, across cultures, there is similarity in intonation, timing, pitch and rhythms?

Observe the interactions between babies and young children in your care:

- *with their parents/main carers. You may have opportunities to do this on a home visit as well as within a setting.*

- *with their Key Person/Early Years practitioner.*

As you observe, whatever age, look for:

- *signs of 'proto-conversations' that have become habitual forms of communication within these special partnerships. The higher pitch of the voice and the slower tone used by the adult make it easier for the baby to follow. These variations have been called motherese or, infant directed speech (IDS) (Doherty and Hughes, 2009, page 236).*

- *any similarities/differences. Can you think of possible reasons for these?*

'Tuning-in': conscious or intuitive?

How does a Key Person for a small group of babies or young children 'tune-in . . . and out' to the differing individual rhythms of rest and stimulation? The last two decades have seen a massive expansion in knowledge and understanding of brain development, from the foetus in utero through the first years of life and on until death. Brain scans are no longer just diagnostic tools for medicine but enable us to fine-tune our knowledge about the workings of the brain and how different areas within it influence aspects of learning. Brain tissue develops or dies throughout life. Increasing awareness of this shows the need to 'use' rather than 'lose' those possibilities, maximising the opportunities for children to develop lifelong social and emotional skills within the first years of life.

A model that is often used as a discussion point when considering connections between emotions, learning and development was developed by Maclean (McNeil, 2009) in 1970, turning around ideas about the way the brain has developed. His 'Tri-une Brain' challenged the general view that the largest, latest to develop area of the brain, the neo-cortex, controlled the other areas. The neo-cortex is associated with reasoning and thinking skills – cognitive intelligence – while the oldest, reptilian area has always been known to maintain systems essential to life, safely secured deep within the brain stem. This includes reflexive stimulation to release adrenalin for flight, fight or freeze responses to danger. Maclean's surprises focused on the third, central limbic system, with its ability not only to control emotions but enable these emotions to impact on the other two areas (Maclean, 1990). McNeil (2009) links Maclean's model with further work carried out in American communities led by Amini. Here the development of this limbic area of the brain was found to be limited without a child/person's experience of unconditional love.

Without limbic resonance a child doesn't discover how to sense with his limbic brain, how to tune-in to the emotional and understand himself with others (Amini et al., 2000, cited in McLean, 2009, page 86). Nerve tissue directly responds to stimulation, so it is in being responsive to social contact with others that neural pathways between the neurons (nerve cells) are created within a young child's brain, enabling them to extend their relationships. Amini *et al.* make a claim here for recognising the importance of *unconditional love and relationship* (McNeil, 2009, page 86) – babies and young children being responded to as they are and having their 'voices' heard. This is seen as a key disposition to learning holistically throughout life. Without a well-developed limbic system to effectively control emotions the thought power of the neo-cortex can just work with the fundamental 'animal tendencies' of the reptilian brain. Whether unconditional love is confined to family relationships or possible within Early Years practice will be discussed further in Chapter 4, but certainly EYPs are expected to *Listen to children, pay attention to what they say and value and respect their views* (EYPS Standard 27). For Early Years practitioners and parents this argument has been reinforced in a key text by Gerhardt (2004) *Why Love Matters – How Affection Shapes a Baby's Brain*. Her systemic approach to understanding how we relate socially and emotionally to each other highlights the critical influences within the first years of life, also impacting on physical and intellectual development – *our earliest experiences as babies have much more relevance to our adult selves than many of us realise* (Gerhardt, 2004, page 10). A baby or young child uses a variety of non-verbal and verbal communication techniques to share their needs/thoughts/aspirations with others. Brain activity is allowing this to happen – linking the reptilian brain (survival needs) with the neo-cortex (thinking, reasoning abilities). Response also generates brain activity, not only in relation to the basic needs/thoughts/aspirations but in creating a 'feeling' of warmth, comfort, satisfaction . . . or frustration, misery, hunger. The activity sets up neural pathways that connect neurons (nerve cells) in the limbic system and will build up as memory banks, relating certain circumstances to positive, neutral or negative results. Babies can only share with others what it is like to be happy, angry or sad by expressing it as best they can in the hope that it can be shared. These are now being acknowledged as intuitive, unconscious responses that tend to be responded to by parents/carers in an intuitive way – 'tuning-in' without thinking about it! An EYP who can also tune-in quickly and interpret the need of a young child correctly, synchronising her behaviour to that of the child, is showing what attachment theorists Schaffer and Emerson call *sensitive responsiveness* (cited in Doherty and Hughes, 2009, page 351).

> *The first three years of life can provide opportunities to make the most of the plasticity of the brain – allowing for variations of experience to mould the templates for socialisation and emotional expression. The right hemisphere (side) is dominant at this time, drawing on the baby and toddler's **unconscious** responses.*

(Schore, 2009)

Schore's ongoing work (1994–) is continually updating knowledge about the importance of positive responses to infant needs as the links develop between the neo-cortex, limbic and brain-stem systems (see Figure 2.1 below). Although messages do pass in the neo-cortex between the right and left sides (hemispheres), allowing for more complex language acquisition, the rapid responses that build up trust and encourage further social and emotional engagement occur in the right hemisphere.

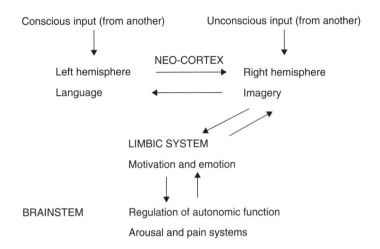

Figure 2.1 Adult (right brain) to infant (right brain) communication: unconscious to unconscious, Allan Schore (2009)

Accurate responses to a baby's message, leading to satisfaction of her or his needs, are likely to strengthen a 'secure attachment' between carer and child. Inaccurate 'mis-cues' may mean a baby remains uncertain about what they are experiencing and whether there is a way to be satisfied – presenting as anxiety, uncertainty and, over time, more likely to be linked to 'insecure attachment'. John Bowlby's theory of attachment (1999) recognised that a familiar pattern of responses to need builds up an *internal working model* within a baby's brain, allowing them to develop behaviour patterns to bring about a response that satisfies them.

The pattern of responses includes facial expression, posture, tone of voice, tempo of movement, physiological changes such as heart rate/body temperature and apparent action, along with strong feelings and emotions. Schore has now been able to show how a caregiver, using right brain **unconscious** skills of: visual – facial messages; auditory – prosodic (patterning, rhythmic) sounds; and tactile – gestural emotional communications can balance out an infant's arousal and emotional state, linking with their right brain. We now know that *the kind of brain each baby develops is the brain that comes out of his/her particular experiences with people* (Gerhardt, 2004, page 38). Schore found that building up the pre-frontal cortex was helped especially through pleasure – joy moments. So, both primary and secondary attachment figures may help each other in understanding the needs of a young child as they *establish fair, respectful, trusting and constructive relationships with families and parents/carers, and communicate sensitively and effectively with them* (EYPS Standard 30).

Many of these behaviours may be intuitive at times and consciously learned and delivered at other times! The latter may draw on the EYP's knowledge and understanding of child development, allowing for informed choice.

Check out the following examples.

- In terms of brief, daily interactions the use of 'No' has immense power to build up trust within a relationship or destroy it. Test out for yourself, or with a partner or colleague,

---

REFLECTIVE TASK

Is 'tuning-in' intuitive?

How does a Key Person for a small group 'tune-in . . . and out' to the differing individual rhythms of rest and stimulation? Further exploration of professional boundaries will occur in Chapters 3 and 4 but, for now, consider whether the ability to 'tune-in' to babies and young children is intuitive, 'consciously learned behaviour' or a combination of both.

Read the text below and compare Trevarthen's recommendations for supporting infants and Standard 25 for an EYP.

The caretaker who enters into intimate, supportive relationships with an infant has to have intuitive, emotional responses and behaviour that are unconsciously controlled and cannot be learned.

(Trevarthen, 1993, page 74).

S25: Establish fair, respectful, trusting, supportive and constructive relationships with children.

In the table below take each 'behaviour' in turn. Complete the table with examples from your own experience of being either intuitive or planned or both.

Behaviour	Intuitive – spontaneous, unconscious reaction	Consciously learned/planned	Both
Smiling	e.g. Responsive to child's chuckles	e.g. Opening welcome	√
Voice-pitching			
Co-regulation of conversation between adult and child			
Snuggling up			
Saying 'No!'			
Responding to a 'Why?' question			
Stroking a child's forehead to settle to sleep			

---

how many different ways it can be communicated, with or without language. Is a head-shake enough to get a safety message across – 'tuning-in' to a potential risk before danger occurs?

- Curiosity is known to be a highly valued learning disposition. So how many 'Why?', 'How?' questions does an EYP working with under 5s 'tune-in' to during a day? Can time be allowed to explore these interests with young children, or are quick answers easier and show how knowledgeable the adult is? Chapter 5 will look at the value of 'sensitive responsiveness' here in terms of the impact of capturing the wonder moments on lifelong learning strategies.

Elfer *et al.* acknowledge some of the challenges for EYPs in accepting the invitation to share *intimacy* (2009, page 50). Babies and young children look for adults to share in their joy and pain, helping them understand and cope with a range of emotions. Are we able to honestly stay with them through pain and discomfort as well as excitement, even in those times we are unable to alleviate the misery? An Early Years tutor was delighted when a

---

PRACTICAL TASK

To 'tune-in', mis-cue or ignore

Babies and children use their voices to make contact and to let people know what they need and how they feel, establishing their own identities and personalities.

(DCSF, 2008a, page 41)

Being acknowledged and affirmed by important people in their lives leads to children gaining confidence and inner strength through secure attachments with these people.

(DCSF, 2008a, page 24)

How prepared are we to empathise with the needs and feelings in babies and young children? For each emotion in the table below think of a time when a baby or young child has displayed this feeling. Identify a 'tuned-in' response then think of an example of how this could be 'mis-cued'. The first six are basic emotions, said to be experienced within the first seven months, followed by five self-conscious *emotions, developing as the child gains an increased sense of* self *(Doherty and Hughes, 2009, pages 341 and 342).*

Emotion	Example from baby/child	Practitioner response 'tuned-in'	Practitioner 'mis-cue'
Happiness	Movement of arms and legs, along with beaming smile and gurgles as food approaches!	'Yes, you're right . . . food's coming . . . you must be hungry . . .'	'You're so pleased to see me . . . let's tidy up before food.'
Sadness			
Anger			
Disgust			
Surprise			
Fear			
Embarrassment			
Shame			
Guilt			
Pride			
Jealousy			

student on work placement said she was loving the 'baby room' experience. However, when asked for a reason it was because, *'the staff are really friendly and sit and chat all day while the babies are on the floor'.* Although sometimes interpreted as laziness, do staff have an underlying fear of fully responding to the inquisitiveness and appeal of a young baby, feeling safer if the 'intuitive' responses are withheld and considered 'unprofessional'? The conditional, conscious, planned responses may seem to be more 'professional' but may limit the quality of learning within Early Years now that we know the impact of positive relationships on cognitive as well as physical, social and emotional development.

EYPs can help children own this range of emotions by 'tuning-in' and empathising (Rogers, 1995, page 115), or is it more comfortable to pretend they are not real? Babies and young children are looking for people to 'cue in' to these powerful feelings, rather than 'mis-cue', which can lead to confusion, mistrust in the other and mistrust in themselves. The ability to express personal feelings and understand the emotions of others is termed *emotional literacy* (Weare, 2004). As leaders and supporters of practitioners, EYPs can also have a role in developing emotional literacy among staff. A recommendation for all Key Persons within a nursery is *having regular opportunities to reflect on the emotional aspects of key working with a skilled, knowledgeable manager or colleague* (Manning-Morton and Thorp, 2001, section 2, page 9). Increasing knowledge of self is covered further in Chapter 3, but picking up the cues quickly is known to help here.

CASE STUDY

Transition

Annaliese (four years old) has just started 'nursery school' in the mornings, having enthusiastically attended full daycare provision, along with her younger brother, since she was two. Because of the distance between these two settings she has also changed to another setting in the afternoons where she can be collected from school. She sounds very sad when asked about her experiences in the afternoon daycare setting. Staff here cannot understand why she does not seem to make the most of the opportunities on offer.

Can you identify potential reasons for A's 'sadness', possibly linking to your own experiences?

What positive, constructive skills/strategies may you recommend to help Annaliese's parents and staff at the afternoon setting 'tune-in' to A's needs?

Gerhardt (2004, page 196) talks about a Responsiveness Cordial for babies, responding to the actual needs of the baby, not what we think they need . . . a tuning-in of just the right amount – knowing when to come in, satisfying that need and when to leave and allow the other to 'be'. Maybe this is true for older children and adults too and could be considered for Annaliese. As well as starting at two new settings, A has left a familiar one. The management of such transitions can provide young children with opportunities to develop strategies for 'resilience' as they cope with change. This becomes a crucial period to build up trust within relationships between A, her family and the different settings. If her 'sadness' can be acknowledged and explored at the beginning, she may be ready to build up new relationships.

Tuning-out

This chapter so far has focused on the intensity of brief, daily interactions. Honesty is essential if trust is to develop within fair, respectful, supporting and constructive relationships between practitioners, primary carers and children. There are time limits to any immediate contact within a relationship, so it is as important to consider 'goodbyes' as much as greetings and ongoing communication. McMullen and Dixon's 'relationship-based approach' to Early Years practice acknowledges the need to be 'mindful' of the moment (see Chapter 1). Babies and young children live in the present, with a growing understanding of people and objects coming and going. Global enjoyment, mixed with

---

REFLECTIVE TASK

'Hello' and 'Goodbye' routines

At the start of a session, children are greeted by Early Years practitioners and say 'Farewell' to parents/carers. Then, at the end of a session, children are greeted by parents/carers and say 'Farewell' to practitioners. Social skills rely on mirror neurons in the brain. Findings about mirror neurons explain how children gain mastery simply from watching, they are etching in their own brains a repertoire for emotion, for behavior and for how the world works *(Goleman, 2006, page 42). 'Social referencing' will also occur as children take their emotional cues from familiar adults at such times, so the way the adults say 'Hello' and 'Goodbye' to each other is significant.*

Look at the table below.

Observe how these events happen for ONE *baby/young child. Look for any similarity in responses between parent and practitioner.*

Then:

Identify various strategies and skills the child will have seen used by these familiar adults. Are there ways an EYP can lead and support other practitioners to value these opportunities with child and parent/carer, promoting positive, trusting relationships?

Child arrives	Child arrives
How does the **parent** say 'Farewell' to the child?	How does the **practitioner** welcome the child?
How does the **parent** say 'Farewell' to the practitioner?	How does the **practitioner** both welcome and say 'Farewell' to the parent?
Child goes home	**Child goes home**
How does the **parent** welcome the child?	How does the **practitioner** say 'Farewell' to the child?
How does the **parent** say 'Farewell' to the practitioner?	How does the **practitioner** both welcome and say 'Farewell' to the parent?
What strategies and skills has the child observed/experienced from above?	What strategies and skills has the child observed/experienced from above?

anxiety, of 'peek-a-boo' through to 'hide and seek'-type activities acknowledge a need for all to play at making sense of these processes. Within Early Years provision there is a variety of opportunities to develop communication skills and strategies through management of farewells, while also valuing consistency.

Personal, Social and Emotional Development is at the front of the *Practice Guidance for the Early Years Foundation Stage* (DCSF, 2008a, pages 26–40), now seen on an equal footing to and, indeed, underpinning the other five areas of learning and development. The Planning and Resourcing column acknowledges not just the importance of communication at the beginning and end of a session, but also when staff change shifts or rooms: *At times of transition (such as shift changes) make sure staff greet and say goodbye to babies and their carers. This helps to develop secure and trusting three-way relationships* (DCSF, 2008a, page 32). These comparatively small interactions play their part in the development of positive, trusting relationships.

C H A P T E R   S U M M A R Y

In this chapter the time and effort spent on 'tuning-in . . . and out' to young children and their families is highly valued. Opportunities have been identified within Early Years settings for 'tuning-in and out' to the everyday 'contingent' needs of babies and young children. The impact of these, sometimes brief, interactions on brain development has been discussed in the light of the current studies of Schore, Trevarthen, Amini and Gerhardt, particularly in relation to ongoing social and emotional literacy. There remains scope to look at the meaning of 'unconditional love' within professional Early Years practice, to be followed up in Chapter 4.

A range of communication skills and strategies allow for 'sensitive responsiveness', maximising opportunities for EYPs to develop secure secondary attachments with children. Intuitive skills are combined with planned, conscious responses, encouraging EYPs to be role-models for effective practice. Inevitably, engaging with powerful emotions can be demanding, so ways for colleagues to gain support from others, or for EYPs to offer support to others, will be addressed in later chapters.

The tasks and case study in this chapter have explored effective ways to nurture children, especially emotionally, in partnership with parents and carers in primary attachments.

Moving on

The supportive and constructive communication skills promoted here are seen as key to establishing the fair, respectful and trusting relationships explored further in the next chapter. Trusting relationships are underpinned by growing trust in oneself as well as in the relationships of self with an ever-extending number of 'others'.

Key sections in the rest of this book will focus on self-awareness in children and the development of self-identity within activities and routines carried out within a variety of settings – full daycare, childminding, pre-school, nursery class.

Reflective activities will help you to identify ways EYPs can lead and support others to *help children become aware of, explore and question differences in gender, ethnicity, language, religion, culture, special educational needs and disability issues* (DCSF, 2008a, page 77).

Self-assessment questions

1 What key scientific studies have shown that the way adults respond to babies' needs and requests impacts on the development of neural pathways in the brain and future learning and development?

2 What is meant by 'sensitive responsiveness'?

3 Can 'sensitive responsiveness' be learnt or is it intuitive, or a mixture of both?

4 How does acknowledgement of feelings/emotions enhance the development of social skills in young children?

5 Identify five ways of 'tuning-in . . . and out' within daily Early Years provision that will help to develop a trusting relationship.

FURTHER READING

Gerhardt, S (2004) *Why Love Matters: How Affection Shapes a Baby's Brain.* London: Routledge.

Goleman, D. (2006) *Social Intelligence.* London: Hutchinson.

McNeil, F (2009) *Learning with the Brain in Mind.* London: Sage.

3 Respect for self and others

Every interaction is based on caring professional relationships and respectful acknowledgement of the feelings of children and their families.

(DCSF, 2008b, 2.1)

CHAPTER OBJECTIVES

The EYFS (DCSF, 2008a) has 'Positive Relationships' as one of its four key themes, along with Unique Child, Enabling Environment and Learning and Development. The underlying principle, or value, stated is that *children learn to be strong and independent from a base of loving and secure relationships with parents and/or a key person* (DCSF 2008a, page 05). The first Principles into Practice card for 'Positive Relationships' is entitled 'Respecting Each Other' and includes under Professional Relationships *if you value and respect yourself, you will do the same for others* (DCSF, 2008b, 2.1).

This chapter will look at ways to 'do' respect, creating and sustaining it through a variety of consistent verbal and non-verbal interactions between Early Years practitioners, children and parents. You should note the challenge of '**every** interaction' in the quote above. The impact of these interactions on the development of a young child's self-identity and self-esteem will be explored.

Key theories, reflective and practical tasks, and the case study in this chapter will link to the following EYPS Standards:

S02: The individual and diverse ways in which children develop and learn from birth to the end of the Foundation Stage and thereafter.

S07: Have high expectations of all children and commitment to ensuring that they can achieve their full potential.

S08: Establish and sustain a safe, welcoming, purposeful, stimulating and encouraging environment where children feel confident and secure and are able to develop and learn.

S13: Make effective personalised provision for the children they work with.

S18: Promote children's rights, equality, inclusion and anti-discriminatory practice in all aspects of their practice.

S19: Establish a safe environment and employ practices that promote children's health, safety and physical, mental and emotional well-being.

S25: Establish fair, respectful, trusting, supportive and constructive relationships with children.

C H A P T E R   O B J E C T I V E S   continued

S26: Communicate sensitively and effectively with children from birth to the end of the Foundation Stage.

S27: Listen to children, pay attention to what they say and value and respect their views.

S28: Demonstrate the positive values, attitudes and behaviour they expect from children.

S29: Recognise and respect the influential and enduring contribution that families and parents/carers can make to children's development, well-being and learning.

S30: Establish fair, respectful, trusting and constructive relationships with families and parents/carers, and communicate sensitively and effectively with them.

After reading this chapter you should be able to:

- define respect in terms of developing relationships;
- acknowledge ways others respect you and the impact this has on your relationships with other adults and children;
- reflect on how the values and beliefs of Early Years practitioners, family, local community and nation can influence the development of a young child's self-identity and self-esteem;
- select respectful responses to children, colleagues and parents throughout the day, acknowledging feelings and including strategies to manage conflict;
- identify ways to lead and support others in their choice of respectful communication skills and co-operative activities which value diversity.

Introduction: what is 'respect'?

What does the term 'respect' conjure up for you? Some individual responses to the question are shown at the end of the chapter. The list of EYPS Standards above may seem long but demonstrates how respect, in direct and indirect ways, should underpin the daily practice of EYPs. You will explore this further in this chapter.

The following definitions connect respect with relationships and will be taken as a basis for exploration and reflection for EYPs. Respect can be seen as *a feeling of admiration for someone because of their qualities or achievements alongside having due regard for the feelings or rights of others* (Compact Oxford English Dictionary, 2008). The previous chapter included giving and receiving **respect** in the form of 'polite greetings'. The aim, now, is to look at ongoing ways to provide respectful responses that will build trust over time and lead to constructive relationships with children, families, parents and carers as stated within the following key EYPS Standards.

S25: *Establish fair, respectful, trusting, supportive and constructive relationships with children.*

S30: *Establish fair, respectful, trusting and constructive relationships with families and parents/carers, and communicate sensitively and effectively with them.*

McMullen and Dixon's relationship-based approach to practice (2009) has three criteria, 'respectful' practice as well as being 'mindful' and 'reflective'. They state: *a relationship-based approach is one that values and respects each relationship partner within the multiple spheres of interaction in our own universe of relationships* (McMullen and Dixon, 2009, pages 111 and 112).

In order to be awarded EYPS the EYP has to provide evidence of establishing these respectful relationships.

REFLECTIVE TASK

Achievements and behaviour that lead to admiration and respect

Reflect on the adults and children you come into contact with during one working day. Take a blank sheet of paper and make three lists.

1. *Think of adults and children whose **achievements and behaviour you admire most** and list examples of their behaviour, e.g. always greet me, believe me, spent a long time on constructing a den with others . . .*

2. *List initials for those adults and children who **you don't really know enough about to admire and respect**.*

3. *Think of adults and children whose **achievements and behaviour you disrespect** and write examples of that behaviour, e.g. shout for no reason at children, gossip, often late . . .*

Reflect on the content and length of each list.

- *Identify the impact of those whose achievements and behaviour you admire most on your own personal and professional development.*

- *Identify the impact of achievements and behaviour you find disrespectful on your own personal and professional development.*

This task will be revisited at the end of the chapter.

As well as respect for others, this chapter will explore how self-respect can be promoted, looking at the development of self-identity and self-esteem. An EYP will be involved in creating, for each child and adult, including themselves, a positive 'self-image' that will be respected by all. Colleagues in a setting, or other family members for a childminder, can play an active role in the creation of these positive 'self-images' for each other.

Respect for colleagues

Affirmation is a term used to express positive validation or assertion that something or someone is right. In terms of relationships it is like saying 'You're really OK!' and 'I'm really OK!' In sensory (touch) terms, affirmation of valued existence between two or more people is shown through handshakes or a kiss on one or both cheeks or 'high fives' or hugs expressing 'You're really here!' 'I'm really here!' Of course, this always needs to take into account cultural practices and contexts. These forms of affirmation link with the 'tuning-in . . . and out' processes described in Chapter 2. They also have a cumulative effect over a period of time, building up a sense of individual and group identity.

REFLECTIVE TASK

Being affirmed . . . or not

Early Years practitioners from a range of settings were asked to share ways they had been affirmed or valued during their last working day.

Two thirds could recollect experiences with:

* *colleagues, e.g. entrusted with a new task following training and congratulated on the results;*
* *parents, e.g. thanked for helping a child to settle in over a week;*
* *children, e.g. stretching arms out for a hug.*

One third of the group, though, could remember no such experiences, feeling they were left on their own to carry out daily routines often with very tight timetables and minimal contact with colleagues.

Think of ways, when:

* *you have been affirmed by colleagues, parents and children;*
* *you have affirmed your colleagues, parents and children.*

Examples, sometimes known as 'positive strokes', may include verbal or non-verbal greetings, practicalities like provision of a cup of tea or a tissue, or being recognised for something you can do.

How do these examples or lack of them, impact on your ability to carry out your daily activities as a caring professional? (DCSF, 2008b, 2.1.).

Affirmation needs to be openly received, as well as given, if it is to create the welcoming environment required to meet EYPS Standard 8: Establish and sustain a safe, welcoming, purposeful, stimulating and encouraging environment where children feel confident and secure and are able to develop and learn.

Maslow for adults and children

Maslow's 'Hierarchy of Needs' (see Figure 3.1 below) is often introduced within training programmes in relation to child development. As a framework it can also be used to explore how individual needs are respected. When considered holistically, the satisfaction – or not – of basic physical needs is often expressed through emotions both verbally – *'I feel hungry', 'I feel tired'* – and non-verbally – irritability, tears, eyes closing. Practitioners can develop their own emotional intelligence by becoming more aware of the link between feelings (emotional needs) and physical needs. Positive relationships are built up over time as basic needs of both oneself and others are identified, respected and met if possible. This is as important for adults as children, but as Boeree (2006) states, when discussing Maslow's hierarchy, it is *a little respect that often seems so very hard to get!* The reflective task above may have highlighted ways colleagues are respected by others meeting their basic needs first.

Figure 3.1 Maslow's Hierarchy of Needs (1943, adapted from Boeree, 2006)

The reasons why many of the Early Years practitioners in the reflective task above did not feel valued were because their basic physical and safety needs were being overlooked. They were not feeling cared for by each other, unable to identify any positive examples. When basic physical and safety needs are not being met people feel unloved and not respected. One expectation of the role of EYPs is that they act as *catalysts for change and innovation . . . good listeners and able to tune-into what colleagues know and can do* (CWDC, 2008, page 05). Change and innovation can focus on tuning-in to the physical and safety needs of staff – both as individuals and a team. A respectful approach will put time and effort into meeting those needs practically throughout a working day. This, in turn, will impact on their ability to respect children and parents and will be discussed further in Chapter 6.

Self-respect and self-identity

Self-respect is defined as having *pride and confidence in oneself* (Oxford Compact English Dictionary, 2008) and is important for each EYP, as you provide opportunities for young children to develop a sense of self-respect.

How do children develop self-respect? They will have a formal **identity** in terms of family name, age, sex, ethnicity and general physical characteristics. They then build on this,

Early Years Professionals receiving and showing respect

A group of EYPs from a range of settings joined a day workshop with some practitioners currently on the long, short and full pathways to EYPS. Their basic needs were already respected through the following:

- *planned 'comfort' breaks mid-morning, lunchtime and mid-afternoon;*
- *refreshments mid-morning and mid-afternoon: tea – including herbal option, coffee – including de-caffeinated and a range of homemade biscuits, seeds and fruit available;*
- *drinking water freely available throughout the day;*
- *clear information provided about facilities, fire exits, timings of activities and breaks;*
- *sit-down buffet lunch with vegetarian, vegan options in different space from workshop;*
- *good ventilation and lighting with outdoor options;*
- *comfortable seating;*
- *adequate resource provision.*

In this carefully prepared environment, the boundaries/guidelines they gave themselves for the day were:

- *listen to each other;*
- *keep a sense of humour;*
- *be brave – 'have a go';*
- *respect needs of individuals;*
- *have no fear of 'failing';*
- *work as a team/teams;*
- *CREATE.*

These agreed guidelines became universal behaviour, sometimes unexpectedly, during the day as individual needs were respected. The underlying provision for basic needs meant participants were concentrating on the higher levels of Maslow's hierarchy – self-esteem and self-actualisation needs.

Evaluations at the end of the day included statements such as:

'we used the skills – including respect – which we were reflecting on'.

'everyone . . . seemed chilled, relaxed and went away feeling appreciated.'

The second quote from the group of EYPs ended with the emotional impact of having been respected – 'feeling appreciated'. Could this be an aim, within a relationship-based approach to practice, for the end of each day for staff, children and parents?

becoming aware of themselves as a separate identity – **self-identity.** *A sense of self . . . develops by degrees and is a product of more and more complex understandings* (Maccoby, 1980, page 251 cited in Miell, 1995, page 190). These understandings of **self-identity** in answer to 'Who am I?' include awareness of personal thoughts, emotions and

---

PRACTICAL TASK

Setting boundaries

When care is taken throughout the day to respect staff needs, they are more likely to respect others, parents and children. Staff can work with parents and children to create guidelines and boundaries for their own settings and these are likely to be owned when grounded in daily experience.

- *List your current setting boundaries or ground rules/code of behaviour and compare with those in the case study above.*

- *Can you identify how these boundaries address physical and safety needs of young children, staff and parents in your setting? (Standards 08,19)*

- *On reflection, are there any changes you may now recommend?*

---

abilities and develop through experiences in different environments and over time. Some of the early stages of this growing self-awareness will be addressed in this chapter as they include the ability to compare personal effort and achievement with others. Constructive, encouraging recognition of personal effort and achievement by other children and adults contributes to the development of a positive self-identity leading to self-respect.

Babies, as discussed in the earlier chapters, discover their image within the surroundings and culture they are brought up in. Bronfenbrenner's 'ecological model' (1979) acknowledges that each child brings their uniqueness into relationships within, initially, a micro-system of family and intimate carers. EYPs will seek to continue recognition of this uniqueness, fulfilling EYPS Standard 2: *The individual and diverse ways in which children develop and learn from birth to the end of the Foundation Stage and thereafter* (CWDC, 2008). This has to be complemented by the requirement of Standard 29: *Recognise and respect the influential and enduring contribution that families and parents/carers can make to children's development, well-being and learning* (CWDC, 2008). Unique identities are already influenced by experiences, values and beliefs of other relationships within the surrounding community – the 'meso-system', which, in turn, are influenced by larger establishments such as schools, religious communities and workplaces recognised as being in the 'exo-system'. Finally, a 'macro-system' encompasses daily living in a particular society through national service provision such as health and education, legislation such as the Children Acts 1989, 2004 and the Childcare Act 2006 leading to EYFS (DCSF, 2008a) and customs including national holidays.

The values and beliefs within a country influence the principles written into legislative documentation, such as EYFS (DCSF, 2008a), impacting on opportunities for a young child to develop a sense of identity. Current debate often focuses on the individualistic approach in England – the unique, protected child – which can seem to value possessions and individual rights over seeing oneself as an active citizen within a local community.

Everyday events within their families, settings and local communities therefore provide the background for babies and young children as they seek to answer a key philosophical question 'Who am I?' (S02). Young babies are defining themselves as being separate from

---

Influences on the development of self-identity

EYPs can lead and support others to help children become aware of, explore and question differences in gender, ethnicity, language, religion, culture, special educational needs and disability issues *(DCSF, 2008a, page 77) (S18)*. A child's **identity** contains factual features concerning gender, ethnicity, language, religion, culture, special educational needs and disability issues. The way these features are valued can influence the development of an individual's **self-identity**.

Think about **three** young children in your care.

Can you identify influences on the development of their **self-identity** from:

a) the 'micro-system' – family and close contacts?

b) the 'meso-system' – Early Years settings, schools, local community?

c) the 'exo-system' – parents' workplaces, religious communities, local health and/or social services?

d) the 'macro-system' – current Early Years legislation, political changes, national tradition/cultures?

At what level are **you** influencing the **self-identity** of children?

How can identification of these different influences help you to:

a) respect the views of others? *(S27, S29)*

b) support the development of a positive self-identity for each child, acknowledging their family culture? *(S18, S29)*

---

others with a power to change things. Time to explore their bodies sees them sucking fingers, finding ears, grabbing toes, rolling over, sitting up and attempting to stand and walk. The sensory discovery of other people's noses, mouth and hair adds to the discovery of both 'self' and 'other'. A young child's self-identity is closely bound up with familiar adults, looking to them for confirmation of who they are. The power to change things comes as they experience adult or child responses to their stares, cries, gurgles or pointing.

How does this self-identity develop? Over the last 100 years psychologists and sociologists have explored the process of how children understand the power they have to influence change – agency. The previous chapter discussed the power of 'imitation'. In this process other children or adults are affirming the actions and sounds of the young baby/child, giving them confidence that they are alive, valued and worthy of responding to. As well as mirroring actions the child gains an awareness of how others see them and their behaviour. This helps form self-identity. Cooley (1902, pages 179–85) termed this experience of self-discovery as the *looking-glass self*.

As an EYP you can be instrumental in these respectful responses, as you *have high expectations of all children and commitment to ensuring that they can achieve their full potential* (S7) (CWDC, 2008).

Mirrors and windows also provide the young child with opportunities to identify the impact of their movements and changes of facial expressions. They can begin to see that changes in what they see coincide with the physical experiences of movement. They then have to differentiate between the power they have to alter those images and the way sometimes an 'other' will change in response to them, but not always.

Mirrors can be integrated sensitively throughout the Early Years learning environment. In an infant toddler and pre-school setting in Reggio Emilia, Italy, the following types are described by Smith (1998, page 206) on her visit to the Diana School.

- A huge walk-in pyramid (or kaleidoscope) of mirrors in the piazza.

- Mirror in the dressing-up area.

- Mirror at child eye-level lining the entry way.

- Lots of table-top mirrors.

- A paradoxical series of mirrors in the bathroom.

- A funhouse distorting mirror.

- Tiny mirrors embedded in cement walls outside the school.

CASE STUDY

'Is this me?'

Fourteen-month-old Stephen toddles up to the long mirror on the wall and places both hands flat against it. He grins at his own face. His right hand slides up and down the mirror and his gaze follows his hand and the reflection. Then he moves both hands up and down. He steps to the side of the mirror, hands against the wall . . . then back again, but only half way. A look of confusion crosses his face as he sees half of himself. He turns round to Roger, his Key Person, who smiles saying 'Who's that in the mirror?' and comes over to kneel beside him. Stephen moves his face so it is fully in front of the mirror, then back facing the wall . . . then back to the mirror.

Roger responds, 'There you are . . . gone . . . there's Stephen again.'

The 'game' continues, Stephen finding he can toddle in front of the mirror – then away . . . then back again, with chuckles of delight until he tires and snuggles up to Roger.

The relationship between Roger and Stephen is an example of the following EYFS commitments under Positive Relationships:

2.1 Respecting each other;

2.3 Supporting Learning – warm, trusting relationships with knowledgeable adults support children's learning more effectively than any amount of resources;

2.4 Key Person – a Key Person has special responsibilities for working with a small number of children, giving them the reassurance to feel safe and cared for and building relationships with their parents.

(DCSF, 2008b, Principles into Practice)

The case study above shows how much can be accomplished within every seemingly small, attentive interaction, building up trust between Key Person and child (S02, S19, S25, S26, S27, S28). As Miell says, *We build up our sense of self from the reactions of others to us and how we believe they view us* (1995, page 195).

Gradually this awareness of self-identity includes understanding and ownership of the specific 'me' categories mentioned before under identity, followed by characteristics arising from comparison with others. This stage of recognition of self has been identified by Lewis (1990) as a *categorical self* (Miell in Barnes, ed.,1995, page 195).

Categories included within a growing awareness of self-identity:

- Name   *'I am Amelie'* said confidently (4 years 10 months)

- Age   *'I'm three'*

- Appearance   *'Look . . . . hurt finger'*, showing cut on finger to a visitor

- Relationship to others   *'This letter's for my friend Rajvee. I'll put it in her letterbox'* (four year old busily mark-making on a scrap of paper)

- Likes/dislikes   *'Like Jo-Jingles'* (three year old jumps up and down excitedly waiting for a music session) *'Not that phone – don't want that one! – not work'*

- Feelings about themselves   Maybe shown through non-verbal actions requiring adult attempts at recognition
'I think you are excited about going to Jo-Jingles.'
'You sound cross as that phone doesn't work. Do you want the one that does?'

Early Years practitioners are challenged within the EYFS to recognise that *for children, being special to someone and well cared for is vital for their physical, social and emotional health and well-being* (DCSF, 2008a, page 22). The 'Key Person' role emphasises the need for finely tuned adults to get to know the individual identities of their children. The creation with children and families of booklets or 'passports' of individual 'Learning Journeys' can help to identify and respect key characteristics of this 'categorical self'. This process, providing each 'Learning Journey' remains unique, can support the 'specialness' of each relationship (S02, S07, S13, S18, S26, S27, S29).

Self-worth and self-esteem

Early Years practitioners, within their daily interactions, enable young children to see themselves and experience a range of feelings about themselves, creating a sense of **self-worth.** Much of this picture of self will develop within nurturing, caring opportunities in the first five years of life. Children *respond to and thrive on warm, sensitive physical contact and care* and *communicate their needs for things such as food, drinks and when they are uncomfortable* (DCSF, 2008a, pages 97, 98). Different cultures may have a different emphasis on what is important to be identified with, for example gender roles, physical skills, social status or belonging to a particular group or community. The development of self is reliant on the surrounding cultural opportunities and expectations (S18). Identity is socially constructed, tying in with the communication theories of Vygotsky (1978), the social learning theories of Bandura (1977) and the 'ecological model' of development of Bronfenbrenner (1979).

Use of 'me' and 'mine'

The sense of self arises in connection with active striving in the face of obstacles.

(Turner, 1968, page 99 cited in Miell, 1995, page 198)

Do we see the struggle over wanting a toy to always be related to the possession of the object? It may be more to do with trying to come to terms with 'self' and says something about cultural values to do with individual ownership.

The tensions introduced in Chapter 2 within Erikson's stages of development are visible during active, ongoing learning moments, as individuals attempt to work out a balance between their needs /demands and those of others. Early Years practitioners may feel more comfortable in making decisions for young children, but a realistic self-esteem develops when children become aware of both what they can and cannot do. This requires provision of opportunities for 'having a go' as well as asking for help as needed.

What skills does an Early Years practitioner need in order to scaffold a young child's experiences on decision-making in this way, respecting their choices? The ability to read 'cues' has already been discussed (Chapter 2). Alongside this comes the recognition of a child's growing will to be themselves with autonomy being tested against feelings of shame or self-doubt if they cannot do what they are trying to (Erikson, 1994, page 94). They require opportunities to experience small, manageable, achievable tasks. Each new step includes an element of risk-taking, encouraging resilience while rewarding curiosity and willingness to 'have-a-go'. A baby, toddler and young child's active involvement in the process can be encouraged, recognising skills and abilities across all areas of learning. *In day-to-day relationships and interactions . . . the child's understanding of his or her self emerges* (Dunn, 1988, cited in Miell, 1995, page 194).

As an area of self-development the child not only gets to discover who they are – physical characteristics, facts about what they can do, who their relatives and friends are, where they live – but they start to measure these facts against what they discover about themselves, often from others. In this way there is a sense of self-evaluation occurring. EYPs play an active role in this process, whether consciously or not! One of the aims of this text is to increase the conscious awareness of this impact in a way that can promote the development of a realistic, positive sense of self-worth for each child. The stepping stones are really being laid in Early Years so it is important to look at how these are being done. However, it is worth identifying here that a child's recognition of their self-worth can be encouraged holistically, if others admire their achievement and effort.

The EYFS (DCSF, 2008) six areas of Learning and Development allow for recognition of children's abilities and skills within:

- Personal, Social and Emotional Development;
- Communication, Language and Literacy;

- Problem-Solving, Reasoning and Numeracy;

- Knowledge and Understanding of the World;

- Physical Development;

- Creative Development.

Harter (1988) found when older children usually talk about themselves they used the following **categories** of skills and abilities to compare themselves with others.

- Scholastic competence – knowledge, understanding and skills in areas such as literacy, mathematics and science.

- Athletic competence – abilities in sports and games.

- Social acceptance – active members of friendship groups and ability to get on with adults.

- Behavioural control – ability to behave in line with the rules and regulations of schools, groups and local communities as well as with friends.

- Physical appearance – description of size, colour, height, sex, overall looks often in comparison with peers.

(Miell in Barnes, ed.,1995, page 195)

Children may see their identity having different levels of 'worth' in different categories, often arising from opportunities provided by familiar adults/settings.

Praise and encouragement

How are we encouraging a young child's self-worth in relation to the categories that matter to them? Often adults make general praise statements about a young child in front of them, or the opposite 'put-downs'.

Category	Praise statement	'Put-down' statement
Physical appearance	Oh, aren't you pretty!	Ugh . . . you are messy!
Scholastic aptitude	You're so clever!	Don't be so stupid!
Athletic ability	Wow – what a footballer!	You're so clumsy
Social acceptance	You get on with everyone	Go away!
Behavioural control	Good girl/Good boy	Naughty girl/Naughty boy

Praise statements can lose their ability, over time, to help a child evaluate their own achievements and build up a realistic sense of self-esteem in that area. On the other hand, for some children it may be the only recognition they get . . . so they will continue to repeat the same behaviour to get a response rather than moving on.

Statements that are effective in encouraging children are specific and relate to an individual's achievements. EYPs can lead and support others by not only role modelling use of encouragement, but also helping staff and parents to extend their vocabulary in recognition of individual achievement. Respect and admiration for effort as well as accomplishment can be offered across all of the EYFS (DCSF, 2008a) six areas of learning while recognising categories important to children – physical appearance, scholastic aptitude, athletic ability, social acceptance and behavioural control.

PRACTICAL TASK

Praise, 'put-down' or encouragement using 'I' messages

In the table below change the general praise statements to specific constructive, encouraging, respectful responses. 'I' messages are personal statements, sometimes expressing your feelings, showing you are actively involved in what is happening. They can be used to affirm your personal appreciation or concern, building respectful relationships constructively.

General praise or 'put-down' statement	Specific encouraging statement, with possible 'I' message
Oh, aren't you pretty!	*I like the way your bunches have those green ribbons. That looks really pretty.*
Ugh . . . you are messy	*I can see you've been making the most of the paint today.*
You're so clever!	
Don't be so stupid!	
Wow – what a footballer!	
You're so clumsy	
You get on with everyone	
We've had enough of you today	
Good girl/Good boy	
Naughty girl/Naughty boy	
Any other general phrases you have heard in practice:	

Factors that influence the development of a sense of self and **self-esteem** are:

- a match between our aspirations/what we'd like to do and our performance;

- how we are supported and regarded by 'significant others' – people who matter to the child.

(Miell, 1995, page 205)

Levels of self-esteem can vary in relation to different categories, such as physical ability or social skills, and over time. A child may have a strong, positive sense of self-esteem in relation to athletic ability, but low when it comes to scholastic achievement. EYPs can consciously remind themselves, and colleagues, to support children fairly across all categories, taking care not to admire more those achievements that tie in with their personal values and interests.

A sense of self develops initially within the family, so children will bring with them the identity they have within that context. For some that may fit comfortably with what is expected within a setting, but others may experience uncertainty and confusion, having to conform to different routines and norms of behaviour.

Painting

Three-year-old Samantha watched two other children hand-painting on a large sheet of paper placed on a protective sheet on the ground outside. They asked the Early Years practitioner if they could take off their shoes and put their feet in the paint as well, then on the paper. Additional paint was added to more trays and they covered the paper with feet and hand shapes, thoroughly involved. With practitioner help they left the painting to dry and cleaned themselves up as well as the equipment. Samantha just kept watching.

Samantha's parents had previously spoken to the setting manager and her Key Person in front of Samantha, about their concerns in regard to 'messy play'. This was not what they expected Samantha to be doing. They had just been invited to attend an Open Evening on creativity but continued to always send Samantha to the setting in designer clothes, expecting her to arrive home clean and tidy.

What is Samantha learning about her self-identity from her parents and from the children? How can you, as an EYP, help the development of Samantha's self-esteem as she looks for a match between what she'd like to do and her performance? How can you show support while also valuing how Samantha is regarded by her parents?

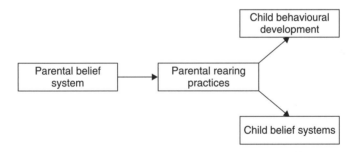

Figure 3.2 The impact of parental belief systems on children's behaviour (Collins in Foley and Leverett, 2008, page 46)

Parents as partners

Parental expectations/belief systems will influence the way parents bring up each child, so will have an influence on the child's beliefs in what is worthwhile. This, in turn, will influence behaviour – both by choice and intuitively. As an EYP gets to know the families and observes interactions with the child/children there is potential to recognise established child-rearing practices and try to understand some of the beliefs behind them. This can help identify similarities between beliefs and practices at home, re-affirming these and hence increasing a child's sense of 'belonging' in different environments. Differences can also be identified, looking for opportunities to constructively work closely with the family and child (S29, S30).

Maccoby and Martin (1983) built on Baumrind's earlier 1973 classification of parenting styles, suggesting four patterns of behaviour that are worth considering in regard to their influence on the development of self-worth in a young child.

PRACTICAL TASK

Effect of parenting styles on behaviour of children
(adapted from Maccoby and Martin, 1983, in Smith et al., *1991)*

In the table below look at the signs of behaviour and attitudes shown by parents who favour specific parenting styles. Many parents combine two or more styles, sometimes using different ones for different children . . . or partners having differing preferences.

Then, write in examples of parent behaviour/attitudes that you have seen which demonstrate a particular style, followed by an example of how the child of that family expresses a sense of self-worth or not.

Style of parenting:	Authoritative	Authoritarian	Permissive	Uninvolved
Signs: behaviour, attitudes *of parents*	Ideas about behaviour and discipline can be explained, discussed and be open to change.	Strict, fixed ideas about discipline and behaviour. Non-negotiable.	Relaxed, undemanding ideas about behaviour.	Uninvolved
	Responsive to children's needs.	Unresponsive to children's needs.	Responsive to children's needs.	Unresponsive to children's needs.
Examples of parenting behaviour you know				
Sense of self-worth for child you know				

REFLECTIVE TASK

How can an awareness of preferred styles of parenting help you as an EYP respect parents and work with them as partners in supporting the identity and self-esteem of their child? (S29, S30)

Research carried out on families where parents had separated found authoritative parenting styles most helped children develop a sense of self-worth (Trinder, 2005). Looking at the behaviour and attitudes in the table above they are most likely to consider the needs of the children and be seen by the children, as they discuss the situation, to be working together.

Impact of personality and temperament on respect for self and others

Personality can be defined as the *differences in the ways in which people relate to objects or other people around them* (Doherty and Hughes, 2009, page 366).

Table 3.1 below shows the five main personality traits and the types of behaviour likely to be demonstrated. An individual can display behaviour from more than one type, but consider the overall descriptions in relation to children you know. Think of behaviour they show in the way they relate to objects or other people.

Table 3.1 Personality types and behaviour

Personality types	Behaviour	Examples of behaviour of child you know
Extroversion	Outgoing Confident Enthusiastic	
Conscientiousness	Responsible Thorough	
Agreeableness	Affectionate Generous Interested in others	
Neuroticism	Anxious Unstable	
Openness	Curious Original	

Temperament describes *constitutionally based individual differences in behavioural style that are visible from early childhood (*Sanson et al., 2004, page 97). A child's temperament is described by Doherty and Hughes (2009, page 367) as a mixture of *core qualities* that create an emotional nature, shown in the way a child responds to situations across areas of development. Although changes will occur throughout life there is an overall stability in the manner of responses, as shown by a study following children from 1½ to 12 years (Guerin *et al.*, 1997, cited in Doherty and Hughes, 2009, page 367). Parent and teacher reports showed similarities in different environments as well as over time. The interest for EYPs is how can children be supported and encouraged to develop strategies in line with their temperament. This may help the development of self-worth.

Thomas and Chess (1986) summarised a range of specific characteristics under three broad groups – 'slow-to-warm-up', 'difficult' and 'easy'.

Parents may often identify different temperaments for their children and are likely to have found different ways of responding to them. Respectful responses seek to value these differences and allow for them within the learning environment in order to provide a 'goodness of fit', 'a match between child-rearing practice and the individual child's temperament', whatever the type (Thomas and Chess, 1977). Chapter 2 included consideration of establishing routines that allowed for the different rhythms of individual children when it comes to satisfying basic needs. Differences in temperament require consideration in the same way throughout the child's day.

Learning how to respect self and others

EYPs are in a position to lead and support by example when it comes to teaching others how to be respectful. Chapter 6 will enable further reflection on the challenges this brings to the individual child. In this chapter it is important to identify ways to help children, colleagues and parents admire each others' achievements, while establishing fair, safe boundaries.

Respect individuals by separating 'behaviour' from the child

Bill Rogers' expertise in behaviour management for children and young people has now been extended to Early Years, drawing on practical experience of his daughter Elizabeth

---

PRACTICAL TASK

From 'Don'ts' to 'Do's'
Rephrase the 'don'ts' as 'do's'

Don't forget to put on an apron before painting

Becomes: *OK, just remember to put the apron on before painting*

Don't push in front of Sami

Becomes:

Don't take the car, Jo needs it

Becomes:

Don't run

Becomes:

Don't fight over the crayons

Becomes:

Don't shout out!

Becomes:

Don't cry . . . you're a big boy/girl now!

Becomes:

McPherson (Rogers and McPherson, 2008). Their analysis of daily interactions between Early Years practitioners and children highlights the effects of different responses on the way a child develops strategies to get on with others. To help children identify the impact of their actions on others the vocabulary and voice tone used to describe these actions is crucial. Very young children are trying to do things for the first time, so descriptive words and encouraging expressions from their carers help them to own the experience. As children experiment with behaviours a skilled practitioner will always comment on the effect of the BEHAVIOUR rather than label the PERSON. Rogers has rated highly the ability of practitioners to provide 'Do . . .' statements and guiding actions that may prevent situations resulting in 'Don't do that!' Some practitioners can also provide humorous comments, defusing tense or frustrating situations. If you, a colleague or child have these skills then value them highly and learn from them! It is important to make sure that you laugh WITH each other, though, rather than be laughing disrespectfully AT someone. There is no place for sarcasm or disrespectful humour.

Mosley (2005a) encourages practitioners to provide opportunities to develop further children's social skills. Young children can learn to make choices which have consequences by directly linking constructive behaviour – 'do's' – with 'don'ts'.

This is demonstrated through her 'Golden Rules' for four year olds upwards:

We listen to people, we don't interrupt

We are honest, we don't cover up the truth

We are kind and helpful, we don't hurt anybody's feelings

We are gentle, we don't hurt others

We try to work hard, we don't waste time

We play well, we don't spoil each others' games

We look after property, we don't waste or damage things.

(Mosley, 2005a, page 4)

Younger children can be introduced to one or two Golden Rules, such as 'we are gentle' and 'we are kind' by using pictures and photographs, along with stories, use of puppets and encouragement within daily activities. Opportunities to talk and play together in small groups, whether in a circle or not, can introduce children to other viewpoints from their own. McTavish (2007) and Sheppy (2009) highlight the use of creativity through stories, puppetry and use of Persona Dolls (Brown, 2001, 2008) to explore the connections between feelings and behaviour. Feelings vocabulary or emotional literacy is being extended through these experiences. The words for feelings are directly linked to facial expressions and appropriate body language, helping children to recognise the meanings of expressions as well as words.

Recognition of conflict

Conflict is part of everyday life as individuals try to satisfy their needs at the same time and in the same place as others! Toddlers and young children are experiencing for the first time outside the family home these complexities of living with others. As mentioned previously, some of the behaviour of adults may fit comfortably with images from home – but not always. Respectful responsiveness acknowledges what has been learnt and seeks ways to extend that learning within the present environment.

Conflict can be identified more accurately through observation of children's facial expressions and body language than listening to voice tone and words. 'Tuning-in' at the first sight of discomfort can be a valued skill of an EYP. However, the young child will also be alert to staff conflict. As Mathieson (2004, page 45) questions, how much attention do Early Years practitioners give to providing consistency between their facial expressions, voice tone, body language and words? This is no easy option, requiring individuals to share such personal feelings as sadness, tiredness and anger in a way that children can recognise the emotion without feeling they are to blame for causing it. Opportunities for Continuing Professional Developmental (CPD) in this area are discussed further in Chapter 7.

A sense of 'genuineness' (Rogers, 1995) comes from this consistency of feelings shown through verbal and non-verbal communication, with young children looking for honest empathy from their carers (see Chapter 2).

Three key questions to focus on when children and adults are involved in conflict are:

1. what is happening? – identify FACTS from all sides;

2. what can we do? – think of at least three different ways to manage the problem;

3. what shall we choose to do now? – agree on one idea to start with, other options can be tried later if that one doesn't work.

Young children can quickly pick up the procedure which involves them in identifying issues and finding solutions (DCSF, 2008a, page 36). Competent role-modelling and ownership by staff and parents recognises the value of time spent listening to different sides of the story and looking for a range of options before making an agreed choice. These seemingly complex co-operative conflict management skills form the basis for a mediation approach to managing conflict, often developed further now within schools and local communities. Respect for all parties underpins this process, so is most effective when supported by the ethos and underlying values of the Early Years setting. Children as young as three or four may be heard managing conflict among their peers, showing that they can:

- listen;
- communicate clearly own needs/wishes;
- appreciate views of others;
- co-operate;
- communicate respect.

(Mathieson, 2004, page 48)

These skills can also be described as assertive, where individuals are confident enough in daily conflict to try out several options together rather than settle for a one-sided decision (S18, S25, S26, S27).

Staff use of assertive strategies to manage conflict helps children own the process. Time to share different strategies can identify a range of communication skills, such as constructive humour and active listening. The willingness to learn from each other can also enhance mutual respect. An example of seeing different viewpoints comes with saying 'sorry!' The full meaning of 'sorry' implies that the speaker fully understands the results of their conscious or unconscious action on another person and chooses to apologise and try not to do it again. In order that the 'sorry' is believed, non-verbal behaviour needs to match the 'sorry', including tone of voice, body position, gestures, proximity and eye contact.

In his development of circle time, White (2008) encourages adults and peers to work together, acknowledging children's as well as adult's rights as active participants with agency to bring about change. Circle activities, when competently facilitated, allow opportunities to practice communication and collaborative skills in a safe environment. They can be used with staff teams as much as with small groups of children but require specific expertise.

What skills and approaches does an EYP need to use to facilitate circle activities to promote mutual respect and skills to alleviate conflict?

1. A real genuine, commitment to the children/adults involved.

2. A non-judgemental attitude – 'no-blame' approach.

3. Active listening and observation skills – being able to 'tune-in' to underlying feelings and create empathy.

4. Keen time management skills – keeping each activity brief while allowing everyone to have a fair share in opportunities to participate if they wish.

5. Boundary-setting.

6. Plan each prepared session, drawing on knowledge of a range of suitable, **fun** activities, but also to be flexible if an unexpected topic or feeling emerges.

7. Containment when emotions run high – whether excitement, anger or distress.

8. Reflection, alone or with others, to help empathic understanding.

All these skills link with the *creation of a growth-promoting climate as they require 'genuineness', 'unconditional positive regard' and 'empathic understanding'*. As Carl Rogers says (1995, page 159), this can help those involved:

- *to take a caring attitude towards themselves;*

- *to listen more accurately to themselves, with greater empathy toward their own . . . vaguely felt meanings;*

- *to be open to . . . new facets of experience which become part of a more accurately-based self concept.*

Supporting relationships

Early Learning Goals (DCSF, 2008a, page 40) state that Early Years practitioners should:

Understand that people have different needs, views, cultures and beliefs, that need to be treated with respect.

Understand that they can expect others to treat their needs, views, cultures and beliefs with respect.

Night and daycare, Sweden – Early Years provision which respects the needs of the community, fathers, mothers, children and setting staff

A group of EYPs visited a range of childcare provision in Sweden. One setting that presented a different angle on parent partnership was staffed 24 hours a day, respecting the needs of some fathers, mothers and children up to the age of 12 within that community. The manager worked with the parents weekly as they found out about their shifts and had to sensitively handle staff rotas to meet their varying needs.

A large hospital and two local factories required shift work with staff on a rota basis throughout 24 hours. The local authority identified a need for childcare for staff, so established a nursery using two floors of a local block of flats and the surrounding outdoor area. The manager had been there for 20 years and developed a range of provision within the nursery – including early years daycare, crèche and breakfast/after school clubs, with older children being collected from several different schools. Along with these was a 'home-from-home' for around 12 children who had bedrooms upstairs.

Respect for them was shown in practical ways such as being able to select their own bedding and towels, names on tooth mugs, towel hooks and bedroom doors, sharing rooms consistently with siblings and toys being left in their rooms with beds made up even if they only came occasionally.

Night staff had a comfortable lounge and kitchen upstairs. The presence of a sewing machine led to the discovery that members of staff were making curtains and other 'homely' furnishings for the nursery.

The outdoor courtyard, as well as being a play area, provided a garden for fruit and vegetables to be eaten in season.

Reflection on the night and day childcare provision

How can 'respecting self and others' be identified as a core value within the provision described in the case study above?

This chapter has focused on the respectful aspect of McMullen and Dixon's 'relationship-based approach to practice' (2009). They suggest, when people are working together, rather than just two sides to a story there is a holistic 'third space'. Here all members of a respectful working relationship have the potential to come away winners and the infants and toddlers and families with whom we work benefit when we engage in an holistic relationship-based approach in dealing with the issues in the day-to-day professional lives (McMullen and Dixon, 2009, page 121). Can the Swedish case study of night and day childcare be an example of this relationship-based approach to practice?

Inclusive practice

Respectful educators will include all children (Nutbrown and Clough, 2006, page 71).

The emphasis throughout this chapter has been on affirmation, communication and co-operative strategies that will respect individuals regardless of additional needs.

To do this it is essential to examine how the *voices* of children are heard and how each *could be said to be included as respected and belonging citizens of their early years communities* (Nutbrown and Clough, 2006, page 71). EYPs, as reflective practitioners, will continually be looking for ways to bring about change to extend and improve their practice. The following is an example of how an EYP is doing just that.

CASE STUDY

Signing with babies and young children

The simultaneous use of spoken and sign language can strengthen the bond and sense of trust between the child and its carers.

(Hill, 2009, page 1)

Geraldine is actively involved in introducing the 'Signs for Success' methodology and practice into her Montessori Nursery School. She continued her own professional development by attending an accredited course that directly impacted on practice – 'Signing with Babies and Young Children' (Robinson, 2008). Over a six-month period, children, parents/carers and Early Years practitioners have become directly involved and the achievements have been 'impressive, rewarding and inspiring'.

This effective practice is now being shared with other local Early Years providers as well as nationally in an Early Years Journal.

Respect leads to respect here as the child's feelings of belonging, being close, acknowledged and accepted are strengthened as it receives audible and visual interaction and praise (Hill, 2009, page 2).

There is a sense of admiration of achievement as signing can be learnt quickly and thus is very empowering for the child – especially for children with English as foreign/additional language (EFL/EAL) and children with special educational needs (Hill, 2009, page 2).

REFLECTIVE TASK

Results from a survey on the use of the above programme in other local areas showed 76 per cent improvement in confidence and self-esteem in babies and young children over six months, as well as documenting the heightened enjoyment of 84 per cent.

The amount of joy in a toddler's relationships appears critical to setting the brain pathways for happiness *(Davidson cited in Goleman, 2006, page 182). This, in turn, leads to greater resilience when under stress.*

Can you identify times of joy within relationships between adults and children and children with each other?

How can you value those moments while respecting the spontaneous personal interactions?

C H A P T E R   S U M M A R Y

This chapter has explored the specific commitment within the EYFS Theme 'Positive Relationships' that centres on 'Respecting Each Other' (DCSF, 2008b).

A priority has been to acknowledge ways others respect you and the impact this has on your relationships with other adults and children. Respectful responses can ripple throughout an Early Years setting during each day, but need to start somewhere, and an EYP has a responsibility to demonstrate *respectful relationships with babies, toddlers, young children, families, colleagues and other professionals* (S25, S30).

Reflective practice has identified how the values and beliefs of Early Years practitioners, family, local community and nation can influence the development of a young child's self-identity and self-esteem. The EYP can continually seek to *recognise and respect the influential and enduring contribution that families and parents/carers can make to children's development, well-being and learning* (S29). This can be helped by identifying different attitudes and beliefs towards bringing up children and looking for ways to work in partnership with fathers, mothers and extended family members in order to encourage a young child to value their self-identity. Examples have shown being respectful as a core element for a 'relationship-based approach' to practice.

The selection of respectful responses to children, colleagues and parents throughout the day will sensitively acknowledge a range of feelings and support individuals as they express these. Creative opportunities such as storytelling or circle-time activities can allow exploration of emotions and include fair, assertive learning strategies to manage conflict.

The role of the Key Person is central to helping a young child develop a secure, trusting secondary attachment, built up through consistent use of respectful responses. This attachment will, in turn, help in the development of a positive self-identity, with a realistic sense of self-worth/self-esteem – an enabling foundation for *making a positive contribution* and *enjoying and achieving* (DfES, 2003).

An EYP can also identify ways to lead and support others in their choice of respectful communication skills and co-operative activities which value diversity, role-modelling *the positive values, attitudes and behaviour they expect from children* (S28). Opportunities may arise to deliver training in relation to the wide range of communication skills and strategies which value respect of self and others, examples of which have been touched on in this chapter.

Moving on

Respecting each other within *every interaction* (DCSF, 2008b) is a challenge and *is based on caring professional relationships* (DCSF, 2008b). The next chapter will identify the need of boundaries for 'care' in order to maintain positive relationships when working with parents as partners, other professionals and young children. These boundaries are especially important for the Key Person. To date, material in this book has looked at ways to own constructive verbal and non-verbal language, promoting social and emotional well-being. These skills and strategies will now be extended to include safeguarding issues and ways to build up resilience during times of transition and stress.

Self-assessment questions

Look back at your response to the first reflective task (page 28). Revisit each question below in turn and identify respectful strategies from this chapter to constructively strengthen these relationships.

1 Think of adults and children whose **achievements/behaviour you admire most.** Identify ways you can affirm/value the behaviour in a way that will develop their self-esteem/self-worth.

2 List initials for those adults and children who **you don't really know enough about to admire/respect.** Identify ways you can affirm/value them just in passing moments during the day.

3 Think of adults and children whose **achievements/behaviour you disrespect** and write examples of that behaviour, e.g. shout for no reason at children, gossip, often late . . . Select respectful, assertive responses that can challenge the disrespectful behaviour.

FURTHER READING

Mosley, J and Sonnet, H (2001) *Here We Go Round – Quality Circle Time for 3–5 Year Olds.* Trowbridge: Positive Press.

Rogers, B and McPherson, E (2008) *Behaviour Management with Young Children. Crucial First Steps with Children 3–7 Years.* London: Sage Publishing.

Sheppy, S (2009) *Personal, Social and Emotional Development in the Early Years Foundation Stage.* Oxford: Routledge.

White, M (2008) *Magic Circles: Self-esteem for Everyone in Circle Time* (2nd ed.). London: Sage.

Responses to the question asked on page 27:

What does the term 'respect' conjure up for you?

Fair	*Assertive*	*Co-operative*	*Unique*	*Personalised*
Individual	*Diverse*	*Self-esteem*	*Self-identity*	
Considerate	*Safe*	*Appreciation*	*Admiration*	*Political Party*

4 Understanding relationships with children in the context of professional boundaries

We build our most trusting and productive relationships between and among those individuals with whom we establish a reciprocal feeling that each partner is valued as competent and worthwhile . . . It is through such relationships that infants and toddlers are provided with the optimum opportunities to learn and develop.

(McMullen and Dixon, 2009, page 112)

CHAPTER OBJECTIVES

The development of positive and trusting relationships between adults and children is ongoing within Early Years practice. This chapter will explore the need to have clear professional boundaries to these sometimes intense relationships – acknowledging the role of the EYP within a *team around the child* (Siraj-Blatchford *et al.*, 2007). The deeper the quality of the positive, trusting relationship between child and practitioner, the more likely it becomes that the practitioner may be the person to identify specific needs thus enabling the 'voice of the baby, toddler or child' to be heard by others able to offer support.

Strategies to support an EYP in this demanding role, working with professionals from other disciplines such as health and social care, will be considered, including opportunities for mentoring and supervision. For example, the EYP needs to be familiar with the Common Assessment Framework (DCSF, 2007), including the role of the Lead Professional. The gradual change in government terminology from Child Protection to Safeguarding requires all Early Years practitioners to be responsible for identification of need and have the ability to work with others for the benefit of child and family. At the time of writing, the case of Baby Peter has re-established the need to express and act on concern sooner rather than later (Badman, 2009). As an EYP you are in a position to lead and support colleagues, as well as be directly involved in multi-professional work yourself.

In this chapter, key theories, reflective and practical tasks, and a case study will link to the following EYPS Standards:

S06: The contribution that other professionals within the setting and beyond can make to children's physical and emotional well-being, development and learning.

S20: Recognise when a child is in danger or at risk of harm and know how to act to protect them.

S23: Identify and support children whose progress, development or well-being is affected by changes or difficulties in their personal circumstances and know when to refer them to colleagues for specialist support.

S34: Ensure that colleagues working with them understand their role and are involved appropriately in help-ing children to meet planned objectives.

S36: Contribute to the work of a multi-professional team and, where appropriate, co-ordinate and imple-ment agreed programmes and interventions on a day-to-day basis.

After reading this chapter you should be able to:

- identify professional boundaries for the Key Person role, acknowledging emotional demands while enabling the 'voice of the child' to be heard by others;

- explore how positive and trusting relationships can be maintained when working within a *team around the child*;

- reflect on how 'competent and worthwhile' the EYP can be in a multi-agency workforce, strengthening rela-tionships with children and families.

Introduction: professional boundaries

Respecting each other within *every interaction* (DCSF, 2008b) is a challenge and *is based on caring professional relationships* (DCSF, 2008b). Boundaries for 'care' can help to main-tain positive relationships when working with parents as partners, other professionals and young children. To date, material in this book has looked at ways to own constructive verbal and non-verbal language, promoting social and emotional well-being. These skills and strategies will now be extended to include safeguarding issues and ways to help chil-dren and staff build resilience during times of transition and stress.

Brooker's results of her own research stated genuine 'Ethics of Care' for young children require adults to take their cue from the children: to watch and wait and respond to their preferences, rather than to *know what they need* (Brooker, 2009, page 107). This affirms Gerhardt's suggestion for a *responsiveness cordial*, discussed in Chapter 2, as Early Years practitioners are curiously *mindful of moments* (Gerhardt, 2004, page 196; McMullen and Dixon, 2009, page 110). Within a relationship-based approach to Early Years practice, though, McMullen and Dixon remind us that this mindfulness extends to communication with colleagues and other professionals. This attentive active listening or tuning-in to emotions comes with personal, as well as professional, cost. Listening to sensitive informa-tion requires time and an enabling environment. This service may not be recognised within a job description, taking the place of other planned activities. Tuning-in to powerful emo-tions of others can generate intense emotions in you without a means of release.

Professionals with active listening as part of their job description e.g. counsellors, social workers, will have supervision sessions with trained staff. These sessions help them acknowledge the emotional impact of 'journeys they travel with others'. Supervision ses-sions help individual practitioners to identify their own boundaries for engagement in relationships, enabling them to separate themselves from 'the other', whether baby, young child or adult. At present, provision of such sessions is rare in Early Years practice, the nearest similar activity being mentoring or active reflective learning groups. We will discuss both of these in Chapters 6 and 7.

Professional bodies, such as VOICE, the union for education professionals, ASPECT, the Association of Professionals in Education and Children's Trusts and ATL, Association for Teachers and Lecturers, have tried to help clarify professional boundaries within job descriptions. These are geared to supporting and protecting practitioners, including with regard to relationship issues such as false allegations and bullying. However, specific relationship roles, such as that of the Key Person, are not always covered in the above, so this chapter will reflect on some of the central issues in establishing professional boundaries. Professional boundaries will need to account for the rights of the babies, toddlers and young children as active participants within the relationships. Later in the chapter a section will explore the impact of hearing the voice of the child within a 'listening culture' and respecting confidentiality.

An Early Years practitioner, maybe the Key Person, who is attuned to a child's voice will have a professional responsibility to share this information on behalf of the child, sometimes with colleagues or other professionals as well as parents. This chapter explores specific times that this may occur in relation to additional or special needs in order to enhance provision for the child's holistic learning and development. The aim of all the professionals involved in multi-agency working must be to retain and develop positive and trusting relationships with the child and family, mirrored by their relationships with each other. A huge challenge!

EYPs have responsibilities to lead and support others in establishing safeguarding strategies to prevent abuse, whether it is physical, sexual, emotional or a pattern of neglect, so they have to be alert to abusive relationships. When we reflect on current cases of abuse we become more aware of the necessity to set boundaries with children, families, colleagues and other professionals at the same time as promoting constructive, collaborative communication. We can describe this approach as a 'listening culture' within a 'relationship-based approach' to professional Early Years practice.

REFLECTIVE TASK

What are my professional boundaries?
Consider your own role, as described in your job description, in terms of your close relationships with children.

Below is a list of some of the areas mentioned in the introduction to this chapter. Try to add practical examples of how you behave in relation to those given, acknowledging boundaries set for each area.

Area	Practical examples of boundaries
'Boundaries for care'	*I keep the door ajar when nappy changing*
'Ethics of care'	*I let Siobhan make the first move for a hug*
Confidentiality	*I have kept the secret about Raj's 'new baby sister' as no one else 'needs to know' this at present*
Relationships with individual children	*Child:adult ratio maintained*

Key Person	Role specification – details
'Hearing the child's voice'	*I observed changes in Sam's body rhythm and chatter. Sam seemed unusually lethargic and disinterested today.*
Multi-agency working	*I met with the speech and language therapist today about Sam*
Safeguarding	*I had a discussion of setting procedures at the staff meeting with Safeguarding Officer and Manager*
Professional 'insurance'	*I am a member of a Union. I read the latest newsletter on-line about job descriptions for EYPs*

- *Are there any other boundaries specific to your role?*
- *Do you think that your examples in the list above show how you work within boundaries, and how they support and protect you in a role with babies and young children?*

For children, being special to someone and well cared for is vital for their physical, social and emotional health and well-being *(DCSF, 2008a, page 24).*

The quote, above, from the EYFS highlights a need for children to be 'special' to someone.

- *What does 'being special' mean to you in relation to your practical examples of boundaries?*
- *Can you identify the strengths of your situation?*
- *Are there any areas for development?*

Professional boundaries to respect children

The United Nations Convention on the Rights of the Child (UNCRC), 1989, clearly identified three main principles – the three Ps – underpinning children's rights:

- provision;
- protection;
- participation.

These have been reinforced, following the Green Paper, *Every Child Matters*, 2003, and in legislation, the Children Act 2004 and the Childcare Act 2006. Professional boundaries for all childcare workers have to take into account the five outcomes of ECM. They are: *Be healthy, stay safe, enjoy and achieve, make a positive contribution and achieve economic well-being* (DfES, 2003).

Provision and protection were always the strongest principles behind responsibility to care for babies, toddlers and young children prior to 1989. More recently, children are seen as active participants in their own lives, with agency in their own learning and development. This is changing the dynamics of childcare and education and the professional boundaries and responsibilities of EYPs. The social constructivist theories, which support this view of the child, influence the way professional boundaries are established for all the children's workforce. We will be discussing these theories further in Chapter 5 in the context of

PRACTICAL TASK

Provision, protection and participation

Using the table below take each of the ECM outcomes in turn and consider them in relation to your daily Early Years practice. Place a tick under any children's rights principle of 'Provision', 'Protection' and 'Participation' reference you think is addressed by that outcome e.g. An Early Years setting will make provision for a child to be healthy by ensuring that the basic needs of food, rest, sleep, exercise and stimulation are met.

Provision	Protection	Participation
Be healthy		√
Stay safe		
Enjoy and achieve		
Make a positive contribution		
Achieve economic well-being		

- *Now look back at the reflective task (page 52) and see if these three principles are also evident within your professional boundaries.*

- *Is any principle more evident in your responses than the others? If so, why do you think that is?*

'relational pedagogy'. The Common Core of Skills and Knowledge for the Children's Workforce (DfES, 2005) includes responsibilities of practitioners to ensure the participation of children, as well as covering skills and knowledge that promote 'provision' and 'protection'. The six key areas for skills and knowledge identified for all, including all Early Years practitioners, are:

- effective communication and engagement;
- child and young person's development;
- safeguarding and promoting the welfare of the child;
- supporting transitions;
- multi-agency working;
- sharing information.

For this chapter we will concentrate on the last four areas because they require more specialist communication skills while drawing on the first two areas which link to knowledge and skills discussed in the previous chapters of this book. Effective communication and engagement with babies, toddlers and young children stems from knowledge of child development. This is the expertise the EYP can bring to multi-agency work, along with trusting relationships built up over time with a child and their family. A deep level of respect, coming from quality interactions with a child, will enable an EYP to *have the confidence to represent actively the child or young person and his or her rights* (DfES, 2005, page 14).

How do we listen to and act on 'the children's voice'?

As well as confidence, what else is needed to act as an advocate on a young child's behalf? Carl Rogers (1995, page 115) argues that certain conditions are needed for a relationship where the development of the individual is the goal.

• Genuineness, realness or congruence.

• Unconditional positive regard.

• Empathic understanding.

Along with these personal skills, key professional ones are to *know the boundaries of personal competence and responsibility, know when to involve others, and know where to get advice and support* (DfES, 2005, page 15).

Why is this important? Specific details concerning participation within the UNCRC (1989) are found in Article 12.

• *Every child and young person has the right to express his or her views freely about everything that affects him or her.*

• *The child or young person's views must be given 'due weight' depending on his or her age and maturity.*

• *The child or young person has the right to be heard in all decision-making processes, including court hearings. The child or young person can speak for him or herself, or someone else can speak for him or her.*

The Common Core of Skills and Knowledge highlights ways EYPs can help children develop the communication skills to be able to participate to this extent in decision-making – *give the children or young person the opportunity to participate in decisions affecting them, as appropriate to their age and ability and taking their wishes and feelings into account* (DfES, 2005, page 13). A whole-setting ethos of a *listening culture* (NCB, 2009) can have guidelines allowing time for active listening as a valued part of daily life.

PRACTICAL TASK

A 'listening culture'

The impact of a 'listening culture' on Early Years provision continues to be explored by the National Children's Bureau (NCB) and their Young Children's Voices Network Project (http://www.ncb.org.uk/ycvn accessed 24th May 2010). As well as six Listening as a Way of Life leaflets, they have produced Listening as a Way of Life – Developing a Listening Culture *(2009), accessible on the same website.*

Read the definition below for a 'listening culture' and highlight key points that relate to establishing professional boundaries.

A listening culture is one in which listening to individual experiences and views is identified as a core feature of the setting's approach and ethos. It involves practitioners interacting respectfully with young children and adults and explicitly documenting the listening process,

---

PRACTICAL ACTIVITY continued

including examples of resultant change. It is an environment in which practitioners value the importance of listening, are aware of and reflective about how they listen, and acknowledge and respond to experiences and views without discrimination. We listen to young children, their families and those we work with for a number of reasons:

It nurtures respectful and confident relationships.

It supports and enhances learning and sustained thinking.

It may reveal inequalities

It contributes to quality improvement.

(NCB, 2009, page 1)

'The Listening Cycle' is the model developed by the Young Children's Voices Network for listening to children. Five stages follow on from each other in cyclical form, starting with listen, document, reflect, take action and feedback. Feedback makes the difference between being listened to and feeling listened to – even if children's wishes cannot be met (NCB, 2009, page 2).

- *What may be a challenge for you in using 'The Listening Cycle' within your professional role?*
- *Consider one strategy you can try in order to develop a listening culture that will allow you to feel supported in reflective practice, confident in knowing how best to meet the needs of individual children and able to record children's progress using children's own perspectives (NCB, 2009, page 2).*

The Common Core recognises the need to *appreciate the effect (on practitioners) of witnessing upsetting situations and know how to get support* as well as to *have an understanding of issues related to aggression, anger and violence, and know the appropriate responses to conflict – whether a situation involves an adult, a peer or the child or young person themselves* (DfES, 2005, page 15). Chapter 3 discussed basic skills for setting ground rules and managing daily conflict. Strategies included active participation of young children, helping them to develop a range of assertive communication skills and to develop a positive self-identity within an Early Years setting. The ability to share appropriate responses to conflict within a staff team was also recommended. The aim is to support children as they recognise key emotions and learn how to manage them, key life skills. So, are these life skills useful on transition to school?

CASE STUDY

Infant school exclusions are rising

A recent press article highlighted the following facts from a new analysis of exclusions within nurseries and schools.

Two children under five are suspended from school for assaults on fellow pupils or teachers every hour of the school day.

A 6 per cent rise in pupils under five excluded for violence compared with the previous year.

CASE STUDY continued

2,610 children aged between three and five were suspended last year, 1,650 for assaults on adults and 960 for assaults on classmates as follows:

5 year olds	*1,120 assaults on adults*	*630 on pupils*
4 year olds	*520 assaults on adults*	*310 on pupils*
3 year olds	*20 assaults on adults*	*10 on pupils*

A discussion in the article included the following:

Anyone who watched the BBC One comedy series Outnumbered – where a mother and father are constantly plagued by the behaviour of their three children aged twelve, seven and five – would have an idea of the dilemma facing headteachers.

Headteachers' leaders warned that more and more children were arriving at school incapable of socialising with other children.

Mike Brookes, general secretary of the National Association of Head Teachers said the introduction of the 'nappy curriculum' – laying more stress on the three R's in nursery and early schooling – could have played its part in increasing the pressure on children to behave.

Earlier this week, the Independent revealed how the Government (Labour) is planning to send guidance to all nurseries and childminders advising them to get the youngest boys to take more interest in writing, scribbling and drawing.

He also stated that 'Young children are placed in a very different environment to home when they come to school. School is a place where there are rules and you have to obey them. Sadly, that is not the case in all homes.'

Mr. Gove, then; the shadow Education Secretary (Conservative) said that one of the first acts of a new Conservative government would be to strengthen teachers' powers of restraint against unruly pupils.

(Garner, 2009, page 16)

REFLECTIVE TASK

- *Write down your immediate feelings as you read the above statements.*
- *Reflect on the factual information in relation to your own practice.*
- *What boundaries do you have in place that can:*
  - *prevent assault on both adults and other children?*
  - *manage assaults if or when they occur?*
- *Using Bronfenbrenner's 'ecological systems model', outlined in Chapter 3, identify potential 'drivers' for this increase in aggressive behaviour. From which of Bronfenbrenner's systems do they come?*
- *What is your response to Mike Brookes' comments on the 'nappy curriculum'?*

Adult views come across strongly in the above article, with a sense of negativity in the television portrayal of the vocal children who have plenty of agency. However, there is an underlying awareness that young children may be under pressure to conform to rules of behaviour before they are ready. This stress seems to be aggravated by transition between Early Years settings and nursery schools. Supporting transitions is another key area within the Common Core of Skills and Knowledge (DfES, 2005). The Early Years curriculum in New Zealand, 'Te Whariki', has strong relational elements also owned by the school curriculum, easing transition (Peters, 2009, pages 29, 30).

REFLECTIVE TASK

Transitions

Look at the table below, showing key strands in the New Zealand Early Years curriculum alongside key strands of their school national curriculum. What impact may these strands have on helping staff support children through transition?

Alignment of the key competencies in the school curriculum with 'Te Whariki'

Strands of 'Te Whariki'	Key Competencies in the School Curriculum
Mana whenua – Belonging	Participating and contributing
Mana atua – Well-being	Managing self
Mana aotūroa – Exploration	Thinking
Mana reo – Communication	Using language symbols and texts
Mana tangata – Contribution	Relating to others

(Source: adapted from Ministry of Education, 2006, page 33 in Peters, 2009, page 29)

How can your knowledge of the social and emotional well-being of children in your care be shared during transitions, respecting professional boundaries?

Key Person approach within a setting

Within a 'listening culture' one of the strengths of a Key Person approach (Elfer *et al.*, 2009) is having someone who can be aware of the type of decisions that affect individual children and will be able to plan opportunities for decision making that can be seen as fun and relevant.

For this approach to flourish it is important to ask: *Is there a 'spirit of advocacy' for the children's voice to be listened to and acted upon?* (Elfer *et al.*, 2009, page 31).

The EYFS (DCSF, 2008a, page 22, DCSF, 2008b, 2.4) identifies the role of the Key Person, drawing on solid research evidence from Elfer, Goldschmeid and Selleck (2009). Early Years settings, including childminders, are at different stages of developing the Key Person approach as staff come to terms with the demands of the role. EYPs lead and support others in practice, and, drawing on current research in the field, have the potential to help those undertaking a Key Person role (CWDC, 2008, page 77). EYPs can bring about change through working with others, as the Key Person approach is the *organisational set-up within the setting that makes it all happen* (Elfer *et al.*, 2003, in 2009, page vi). This allows scope for reflective practice, respecting the dynamics of individual staff teams, parents and children.

Boundaries for the Key Person role

For some, this role with individual children may be seen as a secondary attachment, or within multiple attachments. What characteristic features of a primary attachment need to be present – and can this be termed 'love' or 'mutual attraction'? The Key Person will certainly be 'mindful of the moment', whether their children are directly with them or actively involved elsewhere. They will be able to tune-in to passing facial expressions, alert to interests and sensitive to concerns. They will be able to respect child and family as they have spent time getting to know them. As a reflective practitioner there will be ongoing questions to ask in order to adapt to the changing developmental needs of the young child. Important features within the questioning are likely to centre around:

Consistency of the relationship:

- How much attention, holding and caring should come from one person?
- How much time within a day or session is likely to be needed with each child in a key group?
- How many colleagues should share the relationship?
- How long should the relationship last?
- How are differing individual needs of babies and young children met fairly within a key group?

Getting to know the child very well:

- Is knowledge of the child holistic or focused within one or two specialist areas?
- How is knowledge of each child continually increasing?
- How is knowledge shared with family, colleagues and other professionals?
- How is this knowledge passed on during transitions?

Spontaneous interactions which delight both parties:

- What opportunities are available for spontaneity?
- How is 'delight' shown?

PRACTICAL TASK

Secondary attachments – love . . . or not?
Consider the following reasons for not implementing a Key Person approach, taken from the work of Elfer, Goldshmeid and Selleck (2009, pages 8, 9). A colleague shares one of these concerns with you.

PRACTICAL TASK *continued*

- *It brings members of staff too close to a parental role and they risk becoming over-involved.*

- *If children get too close to any one member of staff, it is painful for them if that member of staff is not available.*

- *It can be threatening for parents who may be jealous of a special relationship between their child and another adult.*

- *The Key Person approach is complex to organise and members of staff need to work as a team, not as individuals.*

- *It undermines the opportunities for children to participate in all nursery–community relationships.*

Provide a verbal or written response to each of these concerns, drawing on your knowledge and skills from practice, in favour of the Key Person approach. You may draw on the following excerpts from EYFS (DCSF, 2008a) to support your argument.

A key person has special responsibilities for working with a small number of children, giving them the reassurance to feel safe and cared for and building relationships with their parents. A key person will help the baby or child to become familiar with the setting and to feel confident and safe within it. They will also talk to parents to make sure that the needs of the child are being met appropriately, and that records of development and progress are shared with parents and other professionals as necessary. Even when children are older and can hold key people from home in mind for longer, there is still a need for them to have a key person to depend on in the setting, such as their teacher or a teaching assistant.

(DCSF, 2008a, page 15)

Key Person: the named member of staff with whom a child has more contact than other adults. This adult shows a special interest in the child through close personal interaction day-to-day. The key person can help the young child to deal with separation anxiety.

(DCSF, 2008a, page 22)

Look at your response. Has it referred to love and the emotional depth of the relationship or does it focus on practicalities of management and care? Do we have a vocabulary that acknowledges these intimate relationships that allow for the difference between parenting and caring/educating? Gerhardt (2004, page 196) claims that *love matters* when it comes to the learning and development of young children. Looking at any job description for Early Years staff we are unlikely to see 'ability to love', yet many staff coming for interview for a post, or training, will verbally give the reason that 'they love working with children'. This may sometimes infer that they enjoy being 'loved' and responded to by children, who may come to them in trust. It requires discernment of the employer/interviewer to ascertain the dependency needs of the prospective Early Years practitioner. They will be required to give and receive within relationships with babies, toddlers and young children.

EYPs can play a key role in helping colleagues develop boundaries in their relationships with children within an 'Ethic of Care'. 'Genuine ethics of care' for young children require adults to take their cue from the children: to watch and wait and respond to their preferences, rather than to 'know what they need'. This agrees with Gerhardt's *responsiveness cordial* (2004, page 196). At times this may lead the Key Person into uncomfortable territory as they provide *infinite attention to the other* and discover needs that they themselves are unable to meet (Brooker, 2009, page 107). Within a 'listening culture', as discussed earlier, support may be available from colleagues. Further support services such as mentoring, supervision, or sharing within a reflective learning community will be explored in the final chapter.

REFLECTIVE TASK

Appropriate professional intimacy

Maintaining an appropriate professional intimacy, which every child needs in order to feel special, while keeping an appropriate professional distance, requires emotional work of the highest calibre (Elfer et al., 2009, page 27).

Think back over your experiences with individual children and see where you have drawn the line between behaviour which is 'appropriate professional intimacy' and behaviour where you have kept 'an appropriate professional distance'.

What specific strategies, moving on from the reflective task on professional boundaries (page 52), do you have that work as boundaries to maintain a professional distance?

The Specific Legal Requirements within the EYFS Statutory Framework (DCSF, 2008c, pages 22–40) provide objective statements about behaviour, recognised within established EYFS training programmes. Do your strategies fit within these legal requirements? Do they also relate to emotional intelligence, showing your ability to engage with your own feelings as well as those of the child?

Are there opportunities to discuss the power of emotions within close relationships with colleagues and thus helping individual practitioners to come to terms with challenges and develop their emotional intelligence?

Boundaries and abuse: physical closeness and holding

Some of your specific strategies above may have centred on physical rather than emotional intimacy. Early Years practitioners who have been working with children for years are often amazed at statements within EYFS (DCSF, 2008a) guidelines such as *Remember that some babies may be used to being fed while sitting on the lap of a familiar adult* (page 99) as this would have been considered the normal way to feed, in close contact. These reactions act as a solemn reminder of what has happened within a growing 'blame culture' when it seems safer to minimise risk by adopting the *precautionary principle* (Gladwin and Collins, 2008, page 158). Members of staff may have different ways to hold and touch babies, while always considering the importance of listening to the children's voice. What is crucial is to find out from children themselves what they need.

Example of nursery guidelines on physical touch and holding

Read the nursery guidelines below.

It is important for children to see practitioners interacting and relating to each other in positive ways. In this nursery we positively encourage the staff and children to develop happy secure relations and play together. Our teaching through play policy includes the area of emotional development. The following details the ways in which personal relationships between adults/children are developed.

Through physical contact, such as holding children's hands.

Holding children gently to reassure them.

Cuddling children to express delight in their behaviour.

Tickling them, to gain attention, to respond to their attempts at communication.

To laugh with children when they show excitement, discovery and pleasure in the world.

To smile, make funny faces.

To sit children on your lap, give comfort to them when they are upset and help them to achieve a goal.

To talk about things that can make children and adults happy or sad.

(Ref. St. Stephen's Nursery Centre in East London, in Elfer et al., 2009, page 54)

Create your own guidelines for the ways in which personal relationships between adults and children are developed in your setting in a way that is meaningful to the parents in your community.

CASE STUDY

Men as Key Persons

Sue, the Deputy Manager of a full daycare nursery, was asked by two mothers, who were looking for a place for their toddlers, if Dave, the EYP, could not be allowed to change their child's nappy. She saw each separately and listened to their concerns.

One mother had been taken aback seeing Dave in the toddler room, saying she 'hadn't thought about men in the nursery'. She said she had full responsibility for her daughter at home and had thought another woman would be doing all the care, especially the 'intimate care'. Sue told her about Dave's work at the nursery over the past four years, including how he had gained EYPS. She went through the nursery guidelines on physical holding and explained that it was not the nursery's policy to allow individual staff to carry out nappy changing behind closed doors on their own. The mother was given the option to stay in the toddler room for a while, be introduced to Dave and observe a session.

Having done this she was able to make an informed decision that she would be happy to fit in with the usual nursery routines, including Dave's active involvement in her child's care. Although Dave was not the child's Key Person (KP) he became the relief person when the Key Person was away, so he carried out full care as needed. This was not a problem for the mother as he had gradually built up a constructive relationship with both the mother and child.

The second mother also had been surprised by Dave's presence. Her family's religious beliefs set clear guidelines on male and female roles in relation to intimate care of babies and young children. She listened carefully to Sue's explanations about nursery procedures and Dave's qualifications and experiences.

After observing a session in the nursery she appreciated Dave's skills with the children in a range of activities and felt better about everything except Dave doing the intimate care. Sue arranged for the two other female staff in the room to take responsibility for this. Dave was still able to build a constructive relationship with the child and family, while accepting and agreeing to the boundaries which respected the family's culture and beliefs.

REFLECTIVE TASK

- *How would you respond to these two mothers?*

- *Identify similarities and differences to Sue's responses.*

- *Are there any strategies you can have in place in preparation for such questions that show respect for religious and cultural beliefs of families while valuing the knowledge, skills and expertise of male EYPs?*

In the above instance, Sue and Dave's professionalism enabled them to work in partnership with both parents, respecting attitudes and beliefs. The honest respectful approach used came from Sue's willingness to engage and actively listen, while building trust with both parents as well as retaining the trust of colleagues.

REFLECTIVE TASK

Nursery worker's abuse of position of trust

Read the following excerpt and reactions, taken from Community Care, 1 October 2009. (The name and address of the nursery and police region have been omitted for ethical reasons.)

'Nursery worker Vanessa George has pleaded guilty to sexually abusing children and distributing indecent images alongside two people whom she met on the internet. George, 39, . . . admitted 13 counts of sexual assault and making and distributing indecent images of children.'

Write down, or share with a friend or colleague, your immediate reaction to the above.

Compare your comments with the reactions, in the same article, from:

REFLECTIVE TASK *continued*

Detective Superintendent Adrian Pearsons, head of . . . Police's Public Protection Unit.

'. . . George carried out dozens of sickening acts on some of the most helpless and innocent children in our society. Each of them held positions of trust in respect of their victims and abused this trust in a calculated and wicked fashion time and time again.'

Right Hon. Ed Balls MP, then Secretary of State for Children, Families and Schools

'It is vital that we find out how an adult could abuse their position of trust in such an evil way and do everything we can to prevent this abuse happening in the future.'

What strategies, as an EYP within a nursery setting, could you:

- *use to try to prevent such abuse happening from within your staff team?*

- *have in place for staff members to intervene if necessary, including involvement of other professionals?*

- *encourage staff to train in skills so that they could support parents and children if such a situation arose?*

The above situation highlights the vulnerability of children and families as they place their trust in Early Years staff. The Safeguarding Vulnerable Groups Act (2006) has led to the development of the Vetting and Barring Scheme (2010). This aims to register adults with the Independent Safeguarding Authority (ISA) who carry out *any activity of a specified nature that involves contact with children or vulnerable adults frequently and intensively*. These sorts of anxieties from parents arise at a time when the Every Child Matters agenda (DfES, 2003), EYFS (DCSF, 2008) and EYPS (CWDC, 2008) are all promoting partnerships with parents. These factors can add to the pressing need for EYPs to clarify boundaries in roles within the setting for the sake of both adults and children.

Professional boundaries with parents and other professionals

> . . . developing and maintaining good multi-agency working is not always easy, but, a team around the child, starting with the child, can create a service that is more responsive to the needs of individual children and their parents and which should give young children the best possible start in life.

(Dame Gillian Pugh in Siraj-Blatchford *et al.*, 2007, page ix)

The focus in this book is on positive and trusting relationships within Early Years settings, but on occasions those relationships benefit from the expertise of others.

Early Years practitioners can play a vital advocacy role on behalf of the baby, toddler or young child. Sharing detailed, informative observations and records may help other services such as Health, Social Services or Speech and Language Services with their provision. EYPs are expected to be able to work collaboratively with families and within multi-disciplinary teams. To maintain trusting relationships with children it is important that EYPs' roles within the multi-disciplinary team are clear and their views are valued accordingly. When EYPs have a close relationship with a child and family it can be extremely difficult and distressing to discover a situation that requires disclosure. Yet following the death of Baby Peter in Haringey in 2007 and the subsequent court case, pressure is back on all staff working with young children to identify and voice concerns immediately and play their part competently within the safeguarding procedures.

REFLECTIVE TASK

Second Serious Case Review of Baby Peter, 2009

Read Badman's 'Conclusion' from the 'Summary of the Second Serious Case Review of Baby Peter' (May 2009), found at http://www.haringeylscb.org/index/news/babypeter_scr.htm.

- *Although Early Years practitioners are not directly involved, highlight actions that impact on Early Years practice.*

This second Serious Case Review reaches a number of important conclusions. It says the actions of the protecting professions were lacking in urgency, lacking in thoroughness and insufficiently challenging to the child's mother.

It says staff adopted a threshold of concern for taking children into care that was too high and had expectations of what they themselves could achieve that were too low.

It is clear from the Serious Case Review that every member of staff in every agency involved with Baby Peter was appropriately qualified, well motivated and wanted to do their best to safeguard him. But his horrifying death could and should have been prevented. The Serious Case Review says that if doctors, lawyers, police officers and social workers had adopted a more urgent, thorough and challenging approach the case would have been stopped in its tracks at the first serious incident. Baby Peter deserved better from the services that were supposed to protect him. It's a dreadful tragedy that he did not receive better protection.

Cases like that of Baby Peter involve problems or raise questions that are not unique to Haringey. The most important lessons from this case need to be learned across Britain and placed in the context of the government's determination to safeguard children. The Laming report and the government's response to it set a new context for child protection in Britain.

I believe the most important lesson arising from this case is that professionals charged with ensuring child safety must be deeply sceptical of any explanations, justifications or excuses they may hear in connection with the apparent maltreatment of children. If they have any doubt about the cause of physical injuries or what appears to be maltreatment they should act swiftly and decisively

- *Consider the challenges of implementing the actions that you have highlighted within Early Years practice.*

- *How can an EYP instigate change using one of those actions which you have highlighted?*

The Common Assessment Framework (CAF)

An Early Years practitioner can instigate additional support, hopefully building on trusting relationships, by completing an initial pre-assessment checklist for the CAF. This simply allows for the expression of concerns about the needs of a baby or young child in the terms of the ECM outcomes – being healthy, safe from harm, learning and developing, having a positive impact on others and free from the negative impact of poverty (DCSF, 2007).

The pre-assessment checklist can be shared with colleagues and parents in order to decide whether to come together with other key professionals to identify how best to provide for the child's needs. The collaborative nature of the CAF process (DCSF, 2007) requires positive relationships from all involved. One of the challenges is to get agreement from parents and all the required professionals. The child, when it is developmentally appropriate, also has to agree to the process. This practice recognises the participatory rights of the child discussed earlier in the chapter. A Key Person may have a highly valued role in enabling the child's views to be heard by being tuned-in to the child's voice and able to share relevant observations. An EYP who is not the named the Key Person within a setting may also be able to fulfil a leading and supporting role here, working with the Key Person and becoming the Lead Professional within the CAF process. For instance, childminders have often been the first to express concern about the well-being of a young child, as in Baby Peter's case, but a childminder may feel they are not being fully heard or valued within a multi-agency team despite their knowledge of the child in question.

PRACTICAL TASK

Sharing the child's voice within the CAF

Within the CAF the four areas below directly relate to relationships. Take each section at a time and think of the type of behaviour of a baby (0–20 months) or toddler (16–36 months) or young child (30–60 months) you may record constructively within each section.

1 Emotional and social development

Feeling special; early attachments; risking/actual self-harm; phobias; psychological difficulties; coping with stress; motivation, positive attitudes; confidence; relationships with peers; feeling isolated and solitary; fears; often unhappy

2 Behavioural development

Lifestyle; self-control; reckless or impulsive activity; behaviour with peers; substance misuse; anti-social behaviour; sexual behaviour; offending; violence and aggression; restless and overactive; easily distracted; attention span/concentration

3 Identity, self-esteem, self-image and social presentation

Perceptions of self; knowledge of personal/family history; sense of belonging; experiences of discrimination due to race, religion, age, gender, sexuality and disability

---

PRACTICAL TASK *continued*

4 Family and social relationships

Building stable relationships with family, peers and wider community; helping others; friendships; levels of association for negative relationships

Identify the sections you were able to contribute most information. At a multi-agency meeting, who may be able to contribute specialist knowledge for other sections?

REFLECTIVE TASK

What skills and knowledge are required to be a Lead Professional?

Look at the skills and knowledge, required for this role, listed below and consider them in relation to the content of this book so far.

Reflect on the skills and knowledge you already have and those you would like to develop.

The core skills identified for success as a Lead Professional are:

- *strong communication skills including diplomacy and sensitivity to the needs of others;*

- *an ability to establish successful and trusting relationships with children, young people and families, and to communicate without jargon;*

- *an ability to empower children, young people and families to work in partnership with other practitioners and to be able to make informed choices about the support they require and receive;*

- *the capacity to support children, young people or parents/carers in implementing a range of strategies to enable them to achieve their potential;*

- *an ability to establish effective and professional relationships with colleagues from different backgrounds;*

- *an ability to convene meetings and discussions with different practitioners;*

- *an ability to translate their own knowledge and understanding into effective practice;*

- *an ability to work in partnership with other practitioners to deliver effective interventions and support for children, young people and families.*

Additionally, the practitioner in the Lead Professional role should draw on:

- *an understanding of other key professionals, and how to contact them for consultation or referral;*

- *knowledge of local and regional services for children and young people, what they offer, and how to contact them;*

REFLECTIVE TASK continued

- *key advocacy skills appropriate to the child or young person's age, understanding and context.*

They will also benefit from sufficient status, authority and credibility to fulfil the role, deriving from:

- *their personal characteristics;*

- *acceptance and respect from other practitioners in relation to the role and functions of the Lead Professional;*

- *clear and transparent systems developed and agreed at strategic level, in relation to line management, accountability, professional support, and escalation routes.*

(www.dcsf.gov.uk/everychildmatters/strategy/managersandleaders/leadprofessional/ skillsknowledge/skills/ accessed 24th May 2010)

The first four core skills relate specifically to material within 'Positive and Trusting Relationships', highlighting the expertise childminders and Early Years practitioners in full daycare, pre-schools and other provision can bring to the *team around the child* (Siraj-Blatchford *et al.,* 2002). The EYP has a specific brief to not only utilise these skills within personal practice but lead and support others to do so – see Chapters 6 and 7.

CHAPTER SUMMARY

The focus within this chapter has been on coming to terms with some of the challenges when developing close, trusting relationships with babies, toddlers and young children. These relationships have continued to be *'mindful of moments'* – responding to the active agency of the child in recognition of participation as well as protection and provision rights. Identification of professional boundaries for Early Years practitioners, especially with the Key Person role, acknowledges emotional demands on staff and aims to establish a sense of supportive security. This should empower staff to continue positive relationships, also enabling the 'voice of the child' to be heard by others on a 'need to know' basis.

Positive and trusting relationships with a child and family require sensitive communication skills if they are to be maintained when working within a 'team around the child'. **Respect** in these initial close relationships has to be mirrored in relationships with colleagues and other professionals. These skills can be developed within practice, with potential for EYPs to provide opportunities to lead colleagues.

Case studies and tasks have identified situations where an EYP can play an active role, both within an Early Years setting and as part of a 'team around the child'. These will continue to require opportunities to **reflect** on how *competent and worthwhile* the EYP can be in a multi-agency workforce, strengthening relationships with children and families.

There is an identified need for leadership and support to encourage and develop emotional intelligence and collaborative communication skills with children and adults, enabling staff to grow in confidence within professional boundaries.

All three elements of McMullen and Dixon's (2009) relationship-based approach to practice – 'mindful', 'respectful' and 'reflective' – have been present when understanding relationships with children in the context of professional boundaries.

Moving on

With increased awareness of the centrality of positive and trusting relationships to Early Years practice there is increased emphasis on *relational pedagogy – learning together* (Papatheodorou and Moyles, 2009). The following chapter will look at trusting relationships as a secure foundation for children's learning.

As the number of EYPs with leadership and supportive skills increases there will be opportunities for CPD. This chapter has highlighted the emotional demands on staff involved in intimate relationships with very young children. Ways to encourage and support staff may include use of services such as mentoring, supervision and coaching, introduced in Chapter 6, while keeping a focus on the main aim of supporting relationships with children.

Further development of knowledge and skills for EYPs in regard to some of the specialist roles, such as Lead Professional, will be a focus for reflection in the final chapter.

Self-assessment question

Having worked through the material in this chapter, create your own definitions, in relation to trusting relationships, for the following:

- 'boundaries for care';
- 'ethics of care';
- Key Person;
- participation rights;
- multi-agency working;
- Lead Professional with CAF.

FURTHER READING

Brooker, L (2009) 'Just Like Having a Best Friend': How Babies and Toddlers Construct Relationships with their Key Workers in Nurseries, in Papatheodorou, T and Moyles, J (eds.) *Learning Together in the Early Years: Exploring Relational Pedagogy.* London: Routledge.

Elfer, P, Goldschmeid, E, Selleck, D (2009) *Key Persons in the Nursery: Building Relationships for Quality Provision.* Oxford: David Fulton Publishers.

Siraj-Blatchford, I, Clarke, K and Needham, M (2007) *The Team around the Child: Multi-agency Working in the Early Years.* Stoke on Trent: Trentham Books.

5 Trusting relationships as a secure foundation for children's learning

Children can confidently build knowledge and take an active role in their own learning when there is a shared experience based on trust, respect and interest.

(Nyland in Berthelsen *et al.*, 2009, page 40)

CHAPTER OBJECTIVES

An EYP is required to *respond appropriately to children, informed by how children develop and learn and a clear understanding of possible next steps in their development and learning* (S14). This chapter explores the increased understanding of the importance of 'relational pedagogy' within Early Years practice. This values trusting relationships as a secure foundation for infants, toddlers and young children to develop affective (emotional) learning dispositions as well as knowledge and skills. Practical examples address interactive learning opportunities linked holistically across the 6 areas of EYFS (DCSF, 2008a) within each EYPS age group: 0–20 months, 16–36 months and 30–60 months. This is then compared with learning opportunities encompassing mixed age grouping, as often in childminding or 'family grouping' situations. Case studies demonstrate the way underlying trusting relationships can lead and support other adults to work with children to build confidence in taking manageable risks in their play (DCSF, 2008a, page 92). Reflective tasks will explore the learning dispositions young children develop within a trusting environment that help to build resilience for the future.

Key theories, reflective and practical tasks and case studies will link to the following EYPS Standards:

S01: The principles and content of the Early Years Foundation Stage and how to put them into practice.

S09: Provide balanced and flexible daily and weekly routines that meet children's needs and enable them to develop and learn.

S10: Use close, informed observation and other strategies to monitor children's activity, development and progress systematically and carefully, and use this information to inform, plan and improve practice and provision.

S11: Plan and provide safe and appropriate child-led and adult-initiated experiences, activities and play opportunities in indoor, outdoor and in out-of-setting contexts, which enable children to develop and learn.

S13: Make effective personalised provision for the children they work with.

S14: Respond appropriately to children, informed by how children develop and learn and a clear understanding of possible next steps in their development and learning.

S15: Support the development of children's language and communication skills.

<table>
<tr><td colspan="2">
C H A P T E R   O B J E C T I V E S   continued
</td></tr>
</table>

CHAPTER OBJECTIVES *continued*

S16: Engage in sustained, shared thinking with children.

S17: Promote positive behaviour, self-control and independence through using effective behaviour management strategies and developing children's social, emotional and behavioural skills.

S22: Give constructive and sensitive feedback to help children understand what they have achieved and think about, evaluate and improve on their own performance.

S25: Establish fair, respectful, trusting, supportive and constructive relationships with children.

S26: Communicate sensitively and effectively with children from birth to the end of the Foundation Stage.

S27: Listen to children, pay attention to what they say and value and respect their views.

S28: Demonstrate the positive values, attitudes and behaviour they expect from children.

S32: Provide formal and informal opportunities through which information about children's well-being, development and learning can be shared between the setting and families and parents/carers.

After reading this chapter you should be able to:

- identify strategies within trusting relationships, using EYFS (DCSF, 2008a), to help babies, toddlers and young children develop constructive learning dispositions;

- critically evaluate how these strategies can be creatively implemented for the three age groups identified for EYPS (2008) as well as mixed age groupings;

- reflect on the growing awareness of the importance of relational pedagogy within Early Years practice and the implications for EYPs.

Introduction

The overview of the welfare requirements within the EYFS begins with the following clear link between learning and positive relationships:

3.1 Children learn best when they are healthy, safe and secure, when their individual needs are met and when they have positive relationships with the adults caring for them. The welfare requirements are designed to support providers in creating a setting which is welcoming, safe and stimulating, and where children are able to enjoy themselves, to grow in confidence and to fulfill their potential.

(DCSF, 2008a, page 14)

Previous chapters have identified strategies and skills to create an emotionally healthy, safe, secure environment where individual needs are responded to within positive, trusting relationships. The importance of routines that cater for children's natural rhythms for food, rest and sleep, physical exercise and eagerness to learn has been discussed. All of these have sought to address EYPS Standards 25–28 concerning relationship with children. They now become the foundation for the more detailed expedition into specific learning opportunities for each age group.

This chapter will now identify how, with these relationships as a foundation, children can have the confidence to 'have a go', acquire dispositions for ongoing learning and be adventurous risk-takers. Learning together in this way will be discussed in terms of *relational pedagogy* (Papatheodorou and Moyles, 2009). This builds on the previously mentioned *relationship-based approach* of McMullen and Dixon (2009) – being 'mindful' of the moment, 'respectful' and 'reflective'. Look out for synergy, that is, an increase in learning opportunities when the energies of adults and children are focused together within activities, with a creative give and take.

What is 'relational pedagogy'?

International perspectives on Early Years provision demonstrate a variety of ways care and education of under 5s has developed, drawing on different cultural expectations and background theories of child learning and development. In England, three different disciplines – health, social care and education – have had their own roles and models in regard to child development, gradually coming together, holistically, under the Every Child Matters agenda (2003) through the CWDC. One result of this fragmented approach has been an individualistic approach to the assessment of children's learning and development. Even within the EYFS practitioners remain observant of individual achievement profiling within each of the six areas.

- Personal, Social and Emotional Development.
- Communication, Language and Literacy.
- Problem-Solving, Reasoning and Numeracy.
- Knowledge and Understanding of the World.
- Physical Development.
- Creativity.

The EYFS (DCSF, 2008a) acknowledges the importance of Personal, Social and Emotional Development and engages with interactive, social learning, parent partnerships and community links. Throughout this chapter tasks will highlight the extensive recommendations for interaction to enhance learning between practitioner and child, as well as between children, and within practitioner and parent interaction, recognising all six areas of EYFS (DCSF, 2008). As an EYP reading this chapter you could build on the discussion in Chapters 1 to 4 and reflect on the quality of those interactions.

PRACTICAL TASK

What do we know about pedagogy and quality interaction in the EYFS?

EYFS documentation (DCSF, 2008) includes a CD-ROM with links to key background research on quality Early Years provision, showing influences on the changes in practice.

*Using the EYFS CD-ROM click on **resources**, then **Positive Relationships**.*

*Explore the range of background articles, reports and websites, but specifically look at the **Research Briefs** and **Research Reports** for:*

PRACTICAL TASK *continued*

- *Researching Effective Pedagogy in the Early Years (REPEY) DfES no. 356*
- *Study of Pedagogical Effectiveness in Early Learning (SPEEL) DfES no. 363*

These detailed studies were carried out for the Department for Education and Skills (DfES) across a range of Early Years settings for three and four year olds, including childminders. They have been instrumental in highlighting the impact on learning of a range of interactive, relationship strategies and skills within positive relationships.

Go into the internet and use the following web addresses to call up the briefs and reports:

REPEY   Brief – www.dcsf.gov.uk/research/data/uploadfiles/RB356.pdf

Report – www.dcsf.gov.uk/research/data/uploadfiles/RR356.pdf

SPEEL   Brief – www.dcsf.gov.uk/research/data/uploadfiles/RB363.pdf

Report – www.dcsf.gov.uk/research/data/uploadfiles/RR363.pdf

***Identify**, just using the 'Briefs', the following key terms:*

- *'sustained, shared thinking' (EYP Standard 16);*
- *'open-ended questioning';*
- *'positive dispositions to learning';*
- *adult 'modelling';*
- *'challenging yet achievable experiences'.*

These terms identify quality in relation to teaching interactions (Siraj-Blatchford et al., 2002) and will be extended within the chapter.

Earlier chapters acknowledged the social child as a member of family, settings, community and country, as with Bronfenbrenner's 'ecological model' of the influence of systems on learning and development. It was noted that some other countries have built this awareness of the child within relationships into their Early Years provision, as with 'Te Whariki' in New Zealand, and the Reggio Emilia Approach in Italy.

REFLECTIVE TASK

Relational pedagogy

Pedagogy has been a term used within education in England and was drawn into the Early Years field through research leading to 'The Study of Pedagogical Effectiveness in Early Learning' (SPEEL). This project focused on effective practice with three and four year olds as the Curriculum Guidance for the Foundation Stage (DfEE, 2000) came into use, and used the following definition of pedagogy:

Pedagogy is both the behaviour of teaching and being able to talk about and reflect on teaching. Pedagogy encompasses both what practitioners actually DO and THINK and the principles, theories, perceptions and challenges that inform and shape it. It connects the relatively self-contained act of teaching and being an Early Years educator, with personal, cultural and communal values (including care), curriculum structures and external influences. **Pedagogy in the Early Years operates from a shared frame of reference (a mutual learning encounter) between the practitioner, the young child and his/her family.**

Compare, now, with that of Theodora Papatheodorou, whose views are drawn from more of an international perspective.

In the case of educating young children, pedagogy means that the adult and the child embark on a journey together. The adult remains the knowledgeable one but that knowledge is facilitative: the adult is the facilitator rather than the one who sets a clearly predetermined path or route. This notion of pedagogy is best reflected in concepts such as the 'zone of proximal development' (ZPD), 'scaffolding' and 'mediation', all of which form central ideas about learning in the Early Years.

(Bruner and Haste, 1987; Vygotsky, 2002; Papatheodorou *et. al.*, 2009, page 4)

- *Reflect on the nature of the relationships between practitioner and child shown in these definitions of pedagogy for Early Years.*

- *Think of a 'mutual learning encounter' you have had with a young child.*

- *Remember a learning 'journey' you started out on with a child, unsure of where it would end.*

- *What age are these children? Are they above or below three years?*

- *Do you feel the term 'relational pedagogy' defines what you do and think as a teacher of under 5s?*

Relational pedagogy and 0–5 Early Years

The SPEEL and REPEY projects focused on practice with three and four year olds, whereas the EYFS and the role of the EYP encompass 0–5 years. Are the positive trusting relationships we are building with babies and toddlers key to Early Years 'pedagogy', that is, teaching and learning together?

Evidence from brain science

Information from neuroscience (Gopnik *et al.*, 2001) shows clearly that a young child's neural networks are *fired* through loving, *attuned* responses as well as what they see, hear, smell, taste and touch (see Chapter 1). *The brain's energy consumption reaches full adult levels at around two years of age. By three the little child's brain is actually twice as active as an adult's brain. Preschool children have brains that are literally more active, more connected and much more flexible than ours* (Gopnik *et al.*, 2001, page 186). A selective process then occurs, strengthening the synaptic connections between nerve cells that provide the messages the child needs most while losing those not needed. The older child and adult becomes a specialist in their own environment/culture through the highly flexible/plastic brain. Children are continually forming *representations* of sounds and patterns drawn from their environments and the brain is learning (reprogramming) as it tries to strengthen the most important connections. However, Gopnik *et al.* (2001, pages 196–97) also states that *the brain seems to love to learn from other people . . . even as adults . . . when we face new problems, unexpected environments, or unusual inputs, we seem to be able to change the wiring once more.* So, there is physiological evidence that teaching and learning in Early Years is relational for child and practitioner! *The human baby's computational system is really a network, held together by language and love* (Gopnik *et al.*, 2001, page 7).

Child development evidence

Attachment theories, as discussed in Chapters 2 and 4, relate mainly to primary carers within the family but have implications for Early Years practitioners within secondary or multiple attachments. The Key Person for a baby, toddler or young child will seek to build up this close, secure relationship but, unless a childminder, will be working with colleagues to extend learning opportunities. Much of the early learning covered above by Gopnik *et al.* (2001) happens within interactions within the family – primary attachments. Nurture is seen **as** nature – the learning happening naturally within attuned responses between babies and adults equipped to be teachers of the young (Gopnik *et al.*, 2001, pages 7, 8). Examples given relate to those in Chapter 2, such as Gerhardt's *responsiveness cordial* and *mother-ese/parent-ese dialogue*. As an EYP it is important to reflect on what is happening within Early Years at a time when more under-three year olds receive care from outside the family home.

REFLECTIVE TASK

Changing attitudes to child-rearing and learning
Consider the following statements.

Our child-rearing environment has radically changed, but we have not yet worked out how to change what we do in response.

Children, in particular, have suffered a grievous decline in just the goods that are most important to them: adult time, energy and company.

(Gopnik et al., *2001, page 203)*

Reflect on:

- *changes you have noted in the child-rearing environment;*
- *how you provide adult time, energy and company to children;*
- *whether this provision of your human resources can be termed relational pedagogy.*

The first three years of life, looking back at Erickson's (1994, page 94) first three stages, show the extent babies and toddlers learn through trusting relationships. Initially, adults provide the baby with experiences, including the introduction of selected, seemingly appropriate objects to discover. Gradually, the objects are seen independently from the giver, but not before a stage of the young child checking out with the familiar adult that the object is OK. Then comes the significant key learning feature of why some things are all right at times, but not at others – 'testing out' independence/autonomy alongside others.

Piaget, drawing on intense recorded observations of his own three children, clearly identified the hunger of very young children to learn (Piaget, 1951). This led to the constructivist theory of children having inbuilt knowledge from birth continually built on through a strong drive to learn. They actively discover new information, own it and then link to similar experiences at key stages throughout childhood, using processes of assimilation and accommodation. Athey has found ways for Early Years practitioners to be mindful of the moments when patterns of behaviour – schemas – of a child show their learning intentions. *Once in tune with these categories of behaviour, adults have a valuable framework for observing children's actions. Schemas are a way of understanding the learning behaviours of children and, as such, give adults and educators an appreciation of what is currently interesting and absorbing the child* (Fisher, 2008, page 13).

Vygotsky supplemented awareness about this inner drive for knowledge with the recognition of the key role of another, usually parent in the initial stages, within this learning process. They use relevant, clear, specific language and assuring presence with the young child in their field of interest, working within the 'Zone of Proximal Development' described by Vygotsky as *the distance between the actual development level as determined by independent problem solving and the level of potential development as determined through problem solving under adult guidance or in collaboration with more capable peers* (Vygotsky, 1978, page 86). Bruner was able to work with Vygotsky and Piaget's theories, alongside additional research in the 1960s that linked knowledge of biology and evolution with learning and development, valuing cultural impact. Bruner's research, along with Wood, included observations of three year olds learning with parental guidance, and led to the development of 'scaffolding' to help this process.

PRACTICAL TASK

Scaffolding learning
Read the excerpt below:

> One of their investigations involved an analysis of the teaching techniques used by mothers with their three- to four-year-old children. The task was designed to incorporate demands that, according to Piaget's theory, pre-operational children (this age group in Piagetian developmental thinking) would not be able to master. The question was whether, with help, pre-school children could be taught how to do so. The task facing mother and child was to assemble a construction toy made up of twenty-one wooden blocks and an arrangement of pegs and holes to create a pyramid. To learn how to do the task alone, the child had to co-ordinate three different features of the wooden blocks (their size, type of peg or hole, and orientation

of pieces) in order to fit them together. To complete the task, the child also had to pile levels into a size-ordered series.

Children younger than seven could not do the task without help (a finding which is in line with Piagetian theory). However, some children as young as three succeeded in doing it alone after they had been taught by their mothers. In an attempt to characterise what the adult did to support the child's learning, we coined the metaphor of 'scaffolding' to describe their activities. Young children succeeded with help, where alone they failed, because the tutor performed a number of functions which kept the child on task whilst they learned. For example, tutors lured the child into task activity by a variety of tactics, such as showing them how pegs fitted into holes. They often simplified problems facing the child by helping them to select pieces, by showing them how to 're-view' objects by turning them around, and so on. By removing all but the pieces that the child was working on to one side, the tutors removed potential sources of distraction, leaving the child to concentrate on the next step. Where a child overlooked or ignored a feature that needed to be taken into account, the tutor could highlight it by pointing it out or naming it. By such seemingly simple tactics, tutors could keep the child involved in the task activity long enough for them to figure out how to do it for themselves.

Not all attempts at scaffolding succeeded, however. Some teaching strategies were more effective than others. For example, some tutors attempted first to show the child how to do the task before allowing them to have a go for themselves. This strategy over-loaded the child's powers of concentration and often led to complaints, to appeals to have a turn and attempts to leave the situation. Other tutoring strategies relied almost exclusively on verbal instructions such as 'put the little blocks on top of the big ones' which the child could not understand without first being shown what actions such instructions entailed in practice.

The approach to teaching which helped children to learn most about how to do the task involved two main 'rules'. First, when a child was struggling, the tutor immediately offered more help. Conversely, when having been given help, the child succeeded, the tutor attempted to 'fade' or to 'up the ante': they gave less help with the next steps until, eventually, the child was managing the task alone. We termed this aspect of tutoring 'contingent' instruction. Such contingent support helps to ensure that the child is never left alone when he is in difficulty, nor is he 'held back' by teaching that is too directive and intrusive.

(Wood, 1998, pages 99–100)

1. *What functions did the mother carry out to enable the child to eventually build the construction toy?*

2. *What elements of a trusting relationship are evident here, looking at the interactions between adult and child?*

3. *How does this example relate to learning support provided within your setting – is 'scaffolding' evident?*

4. *How does 'scaffolding' fit in with 'adult-initiated' and 'child-centred' learning?*

This example also shows how learning theories have developed from each other – the research process in action. As Wood was quick to point out: *in everyday, naturalistic inter-actions between adults and young children, it is usually the child, rather than the adult, who initiates interactions and sets the shared agenda* (Wood, 1998, page 100).

Around the same time, Rogoff combined the home, setting, community learning potential in her use of *guided participation* to describe the relationship element, key to this chapter.

In guided participation, children are involved with multiple companions and caregivers in organised, flexible webs of relationships that focus on shared cultural activities . . . [which] provides children with opportunities to participate in diverse roles.

(Rogoff, 1990, page 98)

This allows for the many different ways adult–child and child–child interactions occur, highlighting the constructive verbal and non-verbal communication skills required to enable the child to own their achievements.

This certainly supports Bronfenbrenner's 'ecological model' recognition of the impact on learning and development from micro-systems – family, meso-systems – settings and other carers and companions and exo-systems – background culture. Look back at Papatheodorou's definition of relational pedagogy above to see the connections there too.

REFLECTIVE TASK

Social construction and relational pedagogy

- *Reflect on your own practice in terms of the brief links above to Erickson, Piaget, Vygotsky, Bruner and Athey. You may like to follow up references to increase your knowledge of these.*

- *How do you see babies and young children testing out their ideas in your presence because they trust you and your colleagues?*

- *What behaviours have you identified in a baby or young child that may show their current interest in learning more, using Athey's schemas?*

- *Are siblings and peers playing a part in the learning process, as well as parents?*

Combining the examples above, quality relationships seem essential for learning from 0–5 years, so relational pedagogy becomes a justified term. As the extent of Early Years provision for under-fives increases, the EYP as an 'agent of change' is in a prime position to clarify what is required to deliver relational pedagogy in the EYFS.

An EYP is required to provide evidence for Validation of an ability to bring about change within personal practice as well as leading and supporting others in each of the EYP age groupings: 0–20 months; 16–36 months; and 30–60 months. This division of chronological ages ties in with the EYFS division as follows:

EYPS	EYFS
0–20 months	0–11 months
	8–20 months
16–36 months	16–26 months
	20–36 months
30–60 months	30–50 months
	40–60 months

Why have we ended up with these age differentiations? Going back to the initial explanations of the development of services in England for children within education, health and social services, each had/has its own model for child development. Social services use primarily a social or needs model, where their services address specific needs in regard to social and emotional welfare of the babies and young children, along with family needs.

Health services centre around:

- provision of services to cater for arising medical needs, including childbirth and maternity services;

- prevention of ill health e.g. immunisation programme and hearing checks;

- promotion of well-being – health education/health promotion programmes, encouraging active participation of children and families.

These provision, prevention, promotion and participation programmes developed around an original model of child development that highlighted attainment of new skills month-by-month, drawn from the intense work in North America and Europe of Sheridan, *Birth to Five Years: Children's Developmental Progress* (Sheridan *et al.*, 1997). The somewhat rigid specifications have been further developed to encompass a wider range of achievements within a holistic, multi-cultural field, but still underpin the PILESS (Physical, Intellectual, Language, Emotional, Social and Spiritual Development); an acronym for child development used in many Level 3 Childcare, Learning and Development courses (Bruce and Meggitt, 2006, pages 219–31). This programme has sought to draw together the caring and health key elements of Early Years provision with the learning and development focus of education.

Education focused mainly on cognitive/intellectual development, developing a subject-orientated National Curriculum for 5–18 year olds, eventually built around four age-related Key Stages for assessment.

Table 5.1 National Curriculum Key Stages for assessment

Key Stage	Year groups	Ages
Key Stage 1	Years 1–2	5–7
Key Stage 2	Years 3–6	7–11
Key Stage 3	Years 7–9	11–14
Key Stage 4	Years 10–11	14–16

Then the *Curriculum Guidance for the Foundation Stage* (DfEE, 2000) and *Birth to Three Matters* (DfES, 2002) saw this ideology travel down from the statutory school template to cover guidelines for Early Years practice with 3–4 year olds and 0–3 year olds respectively.

The EYFS (DCSF, 2008) has come out of combining expertise from the above models alongside our growing awareness of Early Years education and care in other countries, where there is not the same polarisation within disciplines. Seeing the bigger picture may help to justify why it is important for EYPs on the Validation Pathway to remember to record the age in months for each child as they collect evidence, although this should not detract from the importance of seeing each child as unique and planning appropriately. There is also scope for looking at achievements acquired, especially when working with relational pedagogy, across the age range, for example 4 year olds sharing books with 14 month olds.

REFLECTIVE TASK

Ages and stages approach to child development

Think back over your own experiences within Early Years practice. Acronyms arose to help remember facts within different areas of development, using initials as follows:

Physical, Intellectual, Language, Emotional, Social, Spiritual.

- *Do you draw on a child development framework of PIES, PILES or PILESS and, if so, how does it help you to develop trusting relationships as a secure foundation for children's learning?*

- *If you are not familiar with an ages and stages approach to child development, what model do you use? Does it focus on individual achievements or is there a relationship foundation?*

Development in terms of relationships – using EYFS (2008)

The next sections will explore how essential relationships are as a secure foundation to learning, linked to the different age groups within EYPS – babies, toddlers and young children. Statements from the 'Planning and Resourcing' column of EYFS (DCSF, 2008a, pages 26–116) are used, selected from each of the six areas of learning. Take each age group at a time, getting a feel for the special relationship terms used. Look at the recommendations for planning and resourcing across the six areas of learning.

- Personal, Social and Emotional Development (PSED).

- Communication, Language and Literacy (CLL).

- Problem-Solving, Reasoning and Numeracy (PSRN).

- Knowledge and Understanding of the World (KUW).

- Physical Development (PD).

- Creative Development (CD).

Then respond to the questions, different ones for each group, in terms of a quality social and emotional learning environment.

BABIES (0–20 months)	
Area/Age	**Planning and resourcing**
PSED	
Birth to 11 months	Devote uninterrupted time to babies when you can play with them. Be attentive and fully focused.
	Provide a sofa or comfy chair so that parents, practitioners and young babies can sit together.
	Plan to have times when babies and older siblings or friends can be together.
	Learn lullabies that children know from home and share them with others in the setting.
	Provide a variety of cosy places with open views for babies to see people and things beyond the baby room.
8–20 months	Plan opportunities for talking together in quiet places both indoors and outdoors.
CLL	
Birth to 11 months	Share favourite stories as babies are settling to sleep, or at other quiet times.
	Plan times when you can sing with young babies, encouraging them to join in exploration of their fingers and toes.
8–20 months	Create an environment which invites responses from babies and adults, for example, touching, smiling, smelling, feeling, listening, exploring, describing and sharing.
	Find out from parents the words that children use for things which are important to them, such as 'dodie' for dummy, remembering to extend this question to home language. Explain that strong foundations in a home language support the development of English.
	Discover from parents the copying games that their babies enjoy, and use these as the basis for your play.
PSRN	
Birth to 11 months	Let babies see and hear the sequence of actions you go through as you carry out familiar routines.
8–20 months	Collect number and counting rhymes from a range of cultures and in other languages. This will benefit all children and will give additional support for children learning English as an additional language.
KUW	
Birth to 11 months	Provide a range of objects for babies to explore and investigate textures, shapes and sizes, and pictures or photographs of things associated with regular routines.

8–20 months	Ask parents about significant events in their babies' day and how these are talked about, for example, 'boboes' for sleep or bedtime, 'din-din' for dinner time. Display and talk about photographs of babies' favourite places. Collect and share some stories and songs that parents and babies use at home.
PD Birth to 11 months	Have well-planned areas that allow babies maximum space to move, roll, stretch and explore in safety indoors and outdoors. Plan feeding times so that they take account of the individual and cultural feeding needs of young babies. Remember that some babies may be used to being fed while sitting on the lap of a familiar adult.
8–20 months	Plan alternative activities for babies who do not need sleep at the same time as others do. Provide safe surroundings in which young children have freedom to move as they want, while being kept safe by watchful adults.
CD Birth to 11 months	Make available resources such as soft feathers, silk squares and pom-poms, which offer sensory interest to young babies. Have a variety of familiar toys and playthings that babies enjoy looking at, listening to, touching, grasping and squeezing.
8–20 months	Use your face as a resource when you play pretend games. Vary sensory experiences by placing herbs such as basil, parsley or sage in muslin bags for babies to squeeze or catch with their fingers.

For many candidates on the Early Years Professional Status Pathways to Validation, working directly with this 0–20 month old age group is new or has just played a minimal part in their Early Years practice. Yet, as evidence in previous chapters from neuroscience, developmental psychology and Early Years practice show, respectful, responsive, interactions with competent, familiar adults are crucial to learning. Through these interactions the very young acquire self-identity and awareness of self with others, gaining confidence to explore the ever-increasing world around them. A sound knowledge of attachment theory helps an EYP understand the importance of a relationship between a baby and their Key Person. Some candidates on the Pathways will be visiting baby rooms or individual babies over a relatively short period of time, unless they are continually placed with this age group. This means looking for ways to lead and support the Key People in their specialist roles, rather than intrude into a relationship. There can be ways to work with them, finding out through them what is special for individual children in order to develop an enabling learning environment. In this way, trusting relationships are embedded and valued rather than disturbed.

PRACTICAL TASK

Supporting the Key Person approach with 0–20 month olds

Read through the planning and resourcing examples for this age group taken from EYFS as if you are not in a direct Key Person role (DCSF, 2008).

1. List the communication skills you can demonstrate as you work **with** the Key Person and babies in their group:

   E.g. attentive listening

           fully focused

2. *Identify possible changes to room layout and/or resources you could suggest respectfully to the Key Person that you would be willing to develop, working creatively with them, the babies and parents:*

   E.g. a 'cosy corner' for parents, siblings, practitioners and babies to sit with a range of picture books, background lullaby/rhymes/music options and photos of the babies interacting with others.

TODDLERS (16–36 months)

Area/Age	Planning and resourcing
PSED 16–26 months	Consider ways in which you provide for children with disabilities to make choices, and express preferences about their carers and activities. Ensure resources reflect the diversity of children and adults within and beyond the setting.
22–36 months	As children differ in their degree of self-assurance, plan to convey to each child that you appreciate them and their efforts. Create area in which children can sit and chat with friends, such as a snug den.
CLL 16–26 months	Allow time to follow young children's lead and have fun together while talking about actions such as going up, down or jumping. Plan play activities and provide resources which encourage young children to engage in symbolic play, for example, putting a 'baby' to bed and talking to it appropriately.
22–36 months	Plan to encourage correct use of language by telling repetitive stories, and playing games which involve repetition of words and phrases.
PSRN 16–26 months	Provide collections of objects that can be sorted and matched in various ways. Encourage children, when helping with domestic tasks, to put all the pieces of apple on one dish and all the pieces of celery on another for snacks.

| 22–36 months | Create a 'number rich' environment in the home play area. Introduce numbers as they are used at home, by having a clock, a telephone and a washing machine. |
| | Provide props for children to act out counting songs and rhymes. |

KUW

16–26 months	Find out from parents about their children's interests and discuss how they can be encouraged.
	Plan for inclusion of information from parents who do not speak English.
	Provide culturally diverse artefacts and encourage parents to bring in culturally specific and familiar items from home to share.
	Collect stories that focus on the sequence of routines, for example, getting dressed, asking 'How do I put it on?'
	Develop use of the outdoors so that young children can investigate features, for example, a mound, a path or a wall.
	Give opportunities for talks with other children, visitors and adults.
22–36 months	Build on children's particular interests by adding resources to sustain and extend their efforts.
	Provide opportunities for children to work through routines in role-play, such as putting a 'baby' to bed.

PD

16–26 months	Tell stories that encourage children to think about the way they move.
	Create time to discuss options so that young children have choices between healthy options, such as whether they will drink water, juice or milk.
22–36 months	Plan time for children to experiment with equipment and to practise their skills.
	Be aware of eating habits at home and of the different ways people eat their food. For example, some families use hands to eat and some cultures strongly discourage the use of the left hand for eating.

CD

16–26 months	Make notes detailing the processes involved in a child's creations, to share with parents.
	Introduce young children to light fabric curtains, full-length mirrors and soft play cubes for hiding in, peeping at and crawling through.
22–36 months	Choose unusual or interesting materials and resources that inspire exploration such as textured wall coverings, raffia, string, translucent paper . . .
	Draw on a wide range of musicians and story-tellers from a variety of cultural backgrounds to extend children's experiences and to reflect their cultural heritages.

The division of ages for EYPS allows for a degree of overlap, but it is important that the candidate undertaking one of the Validation Pathways demonstrates their understanding of toddler needs here as compared to babies in the younger age group. What is happening within trusting relationships over these months? The toddler's ability to move increasingly at will, rather than depend on the practical helping hands of others, means space is crucial to practise these new skills. Yet, an air of confusion enters the relationships as the young child may find that they can behave in one way at times with some people, yet others may appear cross in a different situation. Erikson's stages of development see the move through a time of developing autonomy and independence to self-doubt. The two year old is trying hard to make sense of the expanding world as specific language and vocabulary enter into communication skills. Meaning-making is high priority, alongside opportunities to make choices. The neural pathways that have been established in the brain through positive interactions in the first months of life still look for familiar recognition. Increasingly, mistakes should become part of the natural attempts to try out new things. As well as bravely wanting to step out alone, the toddler will look for reassurance from a trusting adult. The constructive end of a temper tantrum, when something has been wanted but not gained, is tears and a cuddle, with recognition of the power of the feelings of frustration rather than a telling-off for being 'naughty'.

For the EYP, coming in to work with this age group can be physically as well as emotionally draining. Trusting relationships can help co-regulate emotions (see Chapters 2 and 6) through empathising with the feelings of the young child, helping them to verbalise the feeling and working with them to find a strategy to cope. As Goleman states *youngsters being exposed to stresses they learn to handle, this mastery becomes imprinted in their neural circuitry, leaving them more resilient when facing stress as adults. Repeating that sequence of fear-turning-into-calm apparently shapes the neural circuitry for resilience, building an essential emotional capacity* (Goleman, 2006, page 185).

CASE STUDY

On the run

Read through the EYFS (DCSF, 2008a) planning and resources for this age group above, then look at the experience below.

An EYP candidate was visiting another Early Years setting to see how they had created their learning environment. Specific attention had been given to the indoor/outdoor flow for the children across the age ranges. The outdoor area was really impressive, with many thought-provoking features and areas providing a range of textures, smells, sounds and visual experiences. The candidate found plenty of 'wow' factors for the young children to engage in exploration and be intently involved in specific activities. Yet, to her surprise, she noted a small group of 30 month olds just ran around all the paths. Their delight seemed to be in running . . . round . . . and round. Although an Early Years practitioner was in the vicinity the children seemed perfectly content to just continue running. This was observed for half an hour.

Reflection on case study

- *What is your immediate reaction to the above experience?*

- *How does it relate to 30 month olds you know?*

- *What does it tell you about the relationship between the practitioner and the running children?*

- *How might observations of these children influence planning?*

Footnote: The EYP candidate's curiosity led to her asking the practitioner about the children. Apparently this had become part of their 'routine' over the last few weeks. All of them lived in high-rise flats with no garden or play area. At this time of the morning they seemed to support each other, as one came out and started running, the other three would join in. The 'delight' was mutual and shared. They would gradually come to an end and go in for a drink, or have one outside. The practitioner said she kept an eye on them, giving a smile at times, but they seemed self-contained with each other. As the EYP left the setting she noted photos of the runners, individually and together, laminated and displayed on the wall in the garden. How does this relate to your earlier reflections?

YOUNG CHILDREN (30–60 MONTHS)	
Area/Age	**Planning and resourcing**
PSED 30–50 months	Provide time, space and materials for children to collaborate with one another in different ways, for example, building constructions. Set, explain and maintain clear, reasonable and consistent limits so that children can play and work feeling safe and secure. Build on children's ideas to plan new experiences that present challenges. Provide activities and opportunities for children to share experiences and knowledge from different parts of their lives with others.
40–60 months	Plan regular short periods when individuals listen to others, such as singing a short song, sharing an experience or describing something they have seen or done. Share stories that reflect the diversity of children's experiences. Involve children in agreeing codes of behaviour and taking responsibility for implementing them. Make time to listen to children respectfully when they raise injustices, and involve them in finding a 'best-fit' solution. Give children opportunities to be curious, enthusiastic, engaged and tranquil, so developing a sense for inner-self and peace.

CLL

30–50 months   Provide opportunities for children whose home language is other than English to use that language.

Ensure that all practitioners use correct grammar.

Help children to predict and order events coherently, by providing props and materials that encourage children to re-enact, using talk and action.

When making up alliterative jingles, draw attention to the similarities in sounds at the beginning of words and emphasise the initial sound, for example, 'mmmmummy', 'shshshshadow', 'K-K-K-Katy'.

Plan to include home language and bilingual story sessions by involving qualified bilingual adults, as well as enlisting the help of parents.

40–60 months   Set up collaborative tasks, for example construction, food activities or story-making through role-play. Help children to talk about and plan how they will begin, what parts each will play and what materials they will need.

Provide for, initiate and join in imaginative play and role-play, encouraging children to talk about what is happening and to act out the scenarios in character.

PSRN

30–50 months   Give children a reason to count, for example, by asking them to select enough wrist bands for three friends to play with the puppets.

Show pictures that have symmetry or pattern and talk to children about them.

40–60 months   Play games such as hide and seek that involve counting.

Use rhymes, songs and stories involving counting on and counting back.

Provide a wide range of number resources and encourage children to be creative in thinking up problems and solutions in all areas of learning.

KUW

30–50 months   Use the local area for exploring both the built and the natural environment.

When out in the locality, ask children to help to press the button at the pelican crossing or speak into an intercom to tell somebody you have come back to the setting.

Invite children and families with experiences of living in other countries to bring in photographs and objects from their home cultures including those from family members living in different areas of the UK and abroad.

40–60 months   Encourage children to speculate on the reasons why things happen or how things work.

Make links with children's experiences to provide opportunities to design and make things, such as a ladder for Anansi the spider (in the West African traditional tale).

Draw on the local community to support projects about the seasons. Tap into knowledge and expertise of local farmers, gardeners, allotment holders and so on.

Use appropriate resources at circle time to enable children to learn positive attitudes and behaviour towards people who are different to themselves.

PD

30–50 months Plan opportunities for children to tackle a range of levels and surfaces including flat and hilly ground, grass, pebbles, asphalt, smooth floors and carpets.

Provide a cosy place with a cushion and a soft light where a child can rest quietly if they need to.

Make equipment available and accessible to all children for the whole of the day or session, if possible.

40–60 months Use whole-body action rhymes such as 'Head, Shoulders, Knees and Toes'.

Plan opportunities, particularly after exercise, for children to talk about how their bodies feel.

Ensure that children who get out of breath will have time to recover.

CD

30–50 months Introduce vocabulary to enable children to talk about their observations and experiences, for example, 'smooth', 'shiny', 'rough', 'prickly', 'flat' . . .

Ensure that there is enough time for children to discuss and appreciate the beauty around them in nature and the environment.

Document the processes children go through to create their own 'work'.

Offer a story stimulus by suggesting an imaginary event or set of circumstances, for example, 'This bear has arrived in the post. He has a letter pinned to his jacket. It says "Please look after this bear". We should look after him in our room. How should we do that?'

40–60 months Introduce language that enables children to talk about their experiences in greater depth and detail.

Be sensitive to the needs of children who may not be able to express themselves easily in English, using interpreter support from known adults, or strategies such as picture cards to enable children to express preferences.

Have a 'holding bay' where 2D and 3D models and works can be retained for a period for children to enjoy, develop or refer to.

Make materials accessible so that children are able to imagine and bring to fruition their projects and ideas while they are still fresh in their minds and important to them.

EYPs, whether having gained the Status or on one of the Pathways, usually have had most experience with this age group, whether in pre-schools, crèches, full daycare settings, independent nursery schools, Children's Centres or childminding. The ethos of the setting can influence the importance of 'relational pedagogy', with planning and resources providing examples similar to those above. It is important to highlight from this selection the range of interactions required. The nature of the communication can make a difference to a child's achievement, as well as impacting on their level of self-esteem – Chapter 3.

EYPS and EYFS value learning and achievement from birth to five years, with potential to extend beyond the chronological age limitation. Knowledge and skills acquired in relation to babies and toddlers can also be constructive with this age group. The first chapter started with a quote: *Each generation begins anew with fresh, eager trusting faces of babies, ready to love and create a new world* (L. De Mause, 2002). By 30 months, each young child is well on the way with their own journey, influenced by their primary attachments and other multiple attachments. They may still be eager and trusting, but they may not and the skilled practitioner needs to be able to: 'tune-in' – Chapter 2; help each child to 'respect themselves and others' – Chapter 3; and possibly be prepared to identify needs which may require additional support – Chapter 4.

These children may be starting at a setting for the first time away from the family home, so trusting relationships in partnership with parents will greatly enrich learning. This is the age for exploration with an ever-increasing physical agility, social awareness, extending vocabulary and curiosity. An EYP can become both a trusted facilitator on a child's journey as well as a modeller of good practice to colleagues, seeking to lead and support others.

PRACTICAL TASK

Encouraging positive learning dispositions

Positive learning dispositions were highlighted in work by Carr, influencing the development of the New Zealand Early Years Education Curriculum 'Te Whariki'.

Blandford and Knowles define learning dispositions as an inner attitude, which can be developed in a setting and predisposes a child to want to and to be able to advance in learning *(2009, page 163). Key learning dispositions are:*

- *motivation;*

- *curiosity;*

- *problem-solving;*

- *reflection;*

- *perseverance in times of difficulty, challenge and uncertainty;*

- *expressing a point of view or feeling;*

- *willing to communicate with others;*

- *creativity;*

- *taking responsibility;*

- *trust and playfulness;*

- *confidence;*

- *courage.*

(Developed from 'Te Whariki' and Dowling, 2005, page 67)

These inner drives enable children to be ready, willing and able to learn. The interactions between child and practitioner, and the quality of their relationship, can encourage the development over a period of time of these dispositions. Can they be identified and assessed? One tool, developed for this, is The Child Involvement Scale (Ferre Laevers, 1994), used in the Effective Early Learning (EEL) project (Pascal et al., 1999). This measures levels of involvement/curiosity against the following criteria:

- *concentration;*

- *energy;*

- *creativity;*

- *facial expression and posture;*

- *persistence;*

- *precision;*

- *reaction time;*

- *language;*

- *satisfaction.*

So, looking at the examples for planning and resources above, how can an EYP model quality practice that will help children gain positive learning dispositions within trusting relationships?

PRACTICAL TASK

Sustained, shared thinking

Read the following section on sustained, shared thinking from the EYFS Principles into Practice card 4.3. (DCSF, 2008b).

In the most effective settings practitioners support and challenge children's thinking by getting involved in the thinking process with them.

Sustained, shared thinking involves the adult being aware of the children's interests and understandings and the adult and children working together to develop an idea or skill.

PRACTICAL TASK *continued*

*Sustained, shared thinking can only happen when there are **responsive trusting relationships between adults and children.***

The adult shows genuine interest, offers encouragement, clarifies ideas and asks open questions. This supports and extends the children's thinking and helps children to make connections in learning.

Sustained, shared thinking requires the positive, trusting relationship skills highlighted in this book. Within those relationships, a constructive strategy is to own open-ended questions that can be adapted to individual and small group situations. Some settings have examples of these questions laminated and displayed around the rooms to encourage visiting adults, parents and students to also use them.

Write an example in your words of a specific occasion you might use each suggested open-ended question.

Open-ended question starter	*Complete in your own words for a specific situation*
Why?	
I wonder why. . .	
Do you wonder why . . .?	
How?	
How can we find out?	
I wonder how that works?	
How can you remember . . .?	
What?	
I wonder what will happen next . . .?	
What do you think will happen next?	
What is a good way to . . .?	
What might happen if . . .?	

Combining age groups

This chapter has provided an opportunity to directly link the specific age groupings within EYFS (DCSF, 2008) to the age groups determined within EYPS. However, it is important to remember the degree of artificiality, as in the 'real world' quality interactions occur across age ranges, leading to learning. Dunn's seminal work, *The Beginnings of Social Understanding* (1988), along with Tizard and Hughes' research *Young Children Learning: Talking and Thinking at Home and at School* (1984), highlighted the richness of dialogue at home, with siblings as well as adults. Childminders can identify with these opportunities. Mention is made, in the planning and resource columns of EYFS (DCSF, 2008) above of looking for opportunities for siblings to meet up within nursery or to consider times for different age groups to be together. This may be an area for EYPs to reflect on and will be considered further in Chapter 7.

C   H   A   P   T   E   R   S   U   M   M   A   R   Y

Trusting relationships as a secure foundation for children's learning implies this should be normal Early Years practice. This chapter started by exploring recent research into the growing awareness of the benefits of relational pedagogy. McMullen and Dixon's model (2009) for a relationship-based approach to practice has continued to underpin the content of material, with further recognition of the need to be *'mindful of moments'*, as well as being *respectful*, in order to provide quality, responsive interactions. The third element – *being reflective* – has also now been seen as a key learning disposition for the children as well as adults.

An opportunity to look at the requirements for EYPS alongside some of the EYFS statements for planning and resourcing has highlighted the extent quality relationships are now embedded within the EYFS. This has arisen from a variety of background research projects and theories. It remains up to EYPs to see how to link theoretical knowledge of the impact of attunement, attachment and sensitive responsiveness to daily practice.

Additional specific strategies have been identified within trusting relationships, using EYFS (DCSF, 2008) to help babies, toddlers and young children develop constructive learning dispositions. Whatever the age, the aim is to share the learning journeys of individuals and groups, bearing in mind we are joining them along the way. Using resources to create a cosy environment to welcome parents, siblings and friends can strengthen the interpersonal relationships. Sustained, shared thinking, using open-ended questions specific to a child's activity, can enrich the learning experience.

Critical evaluation has shown some of the challenges when trying to establish trusting relationships within settings with variations in ethos and expectations. There is further scope to explore the benefits, or not, of mixed age groupings within relational pedagogy.

There is obviously growing awareness of the importance of relational pedagogy within Early Years practice. Possible implications for EYPs will be discussed further in Chapter 7.

Moving on

So far, material in this book has focused mainly on creating positive, trusting relationships and looking at the impact of these on brain development, positive self-identity and learning opportunities. The next chapter will explore how EYPs can lead and support other practitioners in sustaining these relationships over a period of time, when dealing with change and in some challenging situations.

The final chapter will allow for reflection on the growing awareness of the value of relational pedagogy and a relationship-based approach to Early Years practice.

Self-assessment question

Sort out the information below.

Match the name of the researcher/theorist to the model/approach/project with a connecting line.

Theorist/researcher	Research topic/model/approach
Bronfenbrenner	Zone of Proximal Development
Bruner	Child Involvement Scale
Carr	Neurological networks wired by positive interactions
Dunn	Ecological model
Erikson	Scaffolding
Gerhardt	Constructionist – assimilation and accommodation
Gopnik	The beginnings of social understanding
Laevers	Stages of trust vs. mistrust, autonomy vs. shame
Papatheodorou	Love matters
Piaget	Learning dispositions
Vygotsky	Relational pedagogy

FURTHER READING

Fisher, J (2008) *Starting from the Child* (3rd ed.) Maidenhead: McGraw-Hill Education Open University Press.

Gopnik, A, Meltzoff, A and Kuhl, P. (2001) *How Babies Think.* London: Phoenix.

Nyland, B, (2009) The Guiding Principles of Participation: Infant, Toddler Groups and the United Nations Convention on the Rights of the Child, in Berthelsen, D, Brownlee, J and Johansson, E (eds.) *Participatory Learning in the Early Years: Research and Pedagogy.* London: Routledge.

Papatheodorou, T (2009) Exploring Relational Pedagogy, in Papatheodorou, T and Moyles, J (eds.) *Learning Together in the Early Years.* Oxford: Routledge.

6 Supporting other Early Years practitioners to build positive relationships

Trust is a peculiar resource; it is built rather than depleted by use.

Unknown

CHAPTER OBJECTIVES

EYPs are required to lead and support other practitioners in sustaining positive and trusting relationships over a period of time, through dealing with change and in other challenging situations. The aim is to build trust through regular use within staff relationships as well as with children and families. Material in the previous chapters will be developed, linking to the EYFS (DCSF, 2008b) Principles into Practice cards – those directly relating to Positive Relationships:

- 2.1 Respecting Each Other

- 2.2 Parents as Partners

- 2.3 Supporting Learning

- 2.4 Key Person

2.2 and 2.3 are seen as central within a definition of *high quality Early Years provision* (DCSF, 2008a, page 08) but are firmly grounded by the others. Specific attention will also be paid to the leadership characteristics shown *in a continuously improving setting* (DCSF, 2008a, page 08) that directly build and sustain positive relationships.

Key theories, reflective and practical tasks, and a case study will link to the following EYPS Standards:

S01: The principles and content of the Early Years Foundation Stage and how to put them in to practice.

S14: Respond appropriately to children, informed by how children develop and learn and a clear understanding of possible next steps in their development and learning.

S25: Establish fair, respectful, trusting, supportive and constructive relationships with children.

S28: Demonstrate the positive values, attitudes and behaviour they expect from children.

S30: Establish fair, respectful, trusting and constructive relationships with families and parents/carers, and communicate sensitively and effectively with them.

S33: Establish and sustain a culture of collaborative and co-operative working between colleagues.

S34: Ensure that colleagues working with them understand their role and are involved appropriately in helping children to meet planned objectives.

S39: Take a creative and constructively critical approach towards innovation, and adapt practice if benefits and improvements are identified.

By the end of this chapter you should be able to:

- recognise the impact positive relationships can have throughout all aspects of Early Years provision;

- acknowledge the range of staff experience and qualifications within Early Years provision – from childcare students to managers – alongside the varied expertise of Candidates on the different EYPS Validation Pathways;

- identify a range of strategies an EYP can use and develop to lead and support other Early Years practitioners, including mentoring, supervision and modelling;

- reflect on key issues arising in terms of relational pedagogy and the Continuing Professional Development (CPD) of the supportive EYP.

Introduction

Positive and trusting relationships build up over time and have been seen in previous chapters to be an essential ingredient to effective Early Years practice with 0–5 years olds. This chapter acknowledges some of the blocks that can prevent a continuous flow of sensitive, responsive interactions between adults and babies, toddlers and young children.

As a leader and supporter of Early Years practitioners, the EYP needs to recognise the penetration power of positive, trusting relationships and the value of having collaborative working as central to the ethos of a setting, or home in the case of a childminder. Such co-operative communication skills may, or may not, sit comfortably with the management structures in varied provision, whether independent schools, Children's Centres, full daycare provision, pre-schools, crèches or childminding. The EYP will need to identify the most constructive way to lead and support others within their system, while continuing to reflect on ways to improve relationships for the benefits of children, parents and staff. Specific characteristics of leadership and supportive skills to deliver high quality practice will be identified first.

Leading and supporting others in positive relationships

At the time of writing, around 4,000 EYPs have gained the Status, so are gradually infiltrating Early Years practice in many different guises. Each has to find ways to lead and support colleagues on the ground, both as a routine part of practice but also as challenges arise or the next change is encountered! One of the biggest challenges voiced by Candidates on the Pathway is the reluctant willingness and readiness of others to be 'led and supported'. EYPs need to be able to give an assertive explanation of their role, adapted for individual circumstances. For instance, a different explanation may be given if, as a room leader in full daycare, you are able to support the manager in developing a family room and are given leadership of the project, to when a childcare student from the local college comes to you with a complaint of bullying by a colleague when they had tried to implement a messy play activity. Both, though, demand an honest appraisal of who you are, what you can offer and where your boundaries lie. This will be reinforced throughout the chapter.

PRACTICAL TASK

Leading and supporting colleagues

*Identify, from the list below, the roles or positions of Early Years staff and students that **you have led and/or supported in terms of a relationship issue**:*

Owner

Manager

Governor

Deputy Manager

Multi-agency staff

Room leader

Childminder

Early Years practitioner

Student

Parent

Other

- *Who receives most of your leadership and support?*
- *Was support initiated by others or you?*
- *Are they more qualified than you, less qualified, the same, or a mixture?*
- *How do you describe your role to each – is it the same or different?*
- *What are the similarities and differences in the types of support you give?*
- *What challenges, if any, have you met in your journey of leading and supporting?*

Strategies you used for provision of leadership and support may have included communication and co-operative skills, covered in the previous chapters. These will be revisited in terms of adult-to-adult communication, creating, in Roger's terms a 'growth-promoting climate' (see Chapter 1). There are also specific services, such as mentoring, formal interviews and appraisals, which will be covered in terms of empowering positive relationships.

Ongoing reflection will link these strategies to support Early Years practitioners in positive relationships with McMullen and Dixon's *Relationship-Based Approach to Practice* (2009) and Papatheodorou and Moyles' *Relational Pedagogy – Learning Together* (2009).

Characteristics of a leader in terms of relationship skills

The leader who cultivates trust appreciates the team's social and emotional dynamics as much as the task in hand.

(Fineman, 2003, page 66)

Quality Improvement across Early Years provision seeks to ensure a consistently high standard of provision and encourages a continual search for ways to improve the quality of learning, development and care. These are leadership responsibilities and have been flagged up for the EYP as an *agent of change*. Other texts have dealt fully with developing leadership expertise (Whalley, 2008) so the spotlight here will fall on positive relationship skills.

EYFS characteristics of a continuously improving setting recognise that the leader will:

- *have energy, enthusiasm and a principled educational vision;*
- *employ a whole-setting approach, support collaborative working and the collective identification and clear expression of pedagogical objectives related to the EYFS framework that promote achievement for all children;*
- *lead a collaborative learning culture – providing time and space for knowledge-sharing and support for continuous professional development for all staff;*
- *lead and encourage a culture of reflective practice, self-evaluation and informed discussion to identify the setting's strengths and priorities for development that will improve the quality of provision for all children.*

(DCSF, 2008a, page 08)

Each EYP or Candidate working towards EYPS needs to clarify for themselves their own role in regard to leading and supporting others in relation to the points above. The first point can be developed by all, looking out for triggers to inspire the energy and enthusiasm as well as those that overwhelm them. An EYP needs to be able to receive support as well as to offer it.

The extent to which an individual is directly involved in 'collaborative working' within a 'whole-setting approach' will vary, so it is important to identify the nature of the relationships, including any 'power' elements present. Detailed study of these dynamics can be found in Stacey's (2009) book in this series *Teamwork and Collaboration in Early Years Settings.* The best place to start is with ourselves, thinking how ready, willing and able we are to be actively involved with others who may have different views and attitudes about Early Years practice.

For EYPs, one constructive way to lead and support is using EYFS (DCSF, 2008b) as a framework for guiding practice. The Principles into Practice cards can be used as prompts for discussion with individual staff, in small groups or as a basis for a workshop with a setting team. Opportunities can be provided for staff to share their views, facilitated by the EYP, fostering a listening culture (NCB, 2009) rather than a 'right or wrong' dictatorial blame one. The selection of a topic arising from a practitioner's area of interest or concern is most constructive and helps to share the positive language of EYFS, extending knowledge and encouraging a learning environment for all.

However, one of the main challenges, even with a willingness and readiness to learn, seems to be TIME!

REFLECTIVE TASK

Time management for support and leadership

Luff (2009), as she explores the realities of relational pedagogy, recognises the problem for staff, from finding time to write up observations to time to discuss findings and plan creatively with colleagues. The observations are fine, it's time that's the problem . . . We do it at sleep times, times like that but sometimes, like last week when there were staff missing, then you get no time at all.

She continues, hopefully:

If practitioners, and their managers, value time spent looking at and listening to children attentively, discussing what is seen and heard, making links with existing knowledge and investigating possibilities for learning, then observation may become an effective tool for relational pedagogy. It can then form the basis for thoughtful, shared reflections on care and teaching and a foundation for informed action to offer social and emotional support, facilitate playful learning and provide cognitive challenges.

(Luff, 2009, page 73)

- *How does this link to your experience of finding time to discuss practice, link with knowledge of EYFS and other background theories and research and investigate possibilities for learning?*

- *Why may opportunities for thoughtful, shared reflections on care create a foundation for offering social and emotional support, along with facilitating playful learning and providing cognitive challenge?*

Often, EYPs support others most effectively when using a reflective practitioner approach with colleagues to identify areas for development, implement a change and evaluate and reflect on the outcomes. In this constructive way, colleagues end up working collaboratively, leadership and support is facilitative and all involved become empowered, adding to a 'growth-promoting climate'. The leader here demonstrates the skills of:

- genuineness – being themselves while leading and supporting;

- unconditional positive regard – working through a project valuing others' input as it comes, taking 'mistakes' as learning opportunities and not 'blaming' others, accepting and caring for the adults as you would a baby or young child;

- empathic understanding – sensing the feelings of others and using skills to recognise these and work with them.

Such a climate benefits from, and enhances, a 'listening culture' (see Chapter 4 for more detail on this) and the 'leader' will do well to listen and observe the needs of other practitioners, parents and children. Success with support and leadership is more likely to come with a 'contingent response' to a need identified by the 'other' rather than the leader. However, at times, intuitive thinking may play a part in helping out others.

CASE STUDY

Nasra was gaining practical experience in the baby room at a full daycare setting, while undertaking her Pathway towards EYPS Validation. She listened to the concerns of two of the staff members as they were trying to implement EYFS. They felt there was limited provision for staff or parents to sit comfortably with the babies, some of whom were now starting to crawl and walk a few steps. She asked if she could help, sharing a willingness to ask the parents if they had any ideas too. Before she knew it, she was leading a project!

She spoke informally to parents as they collected their children, just letting them know what the practitioners were considering so that they were aware of her interest. Then she created a brief questionnaire saying what was available at present, asking what parents and staff thought about a few ideas and leaving space for them to add more. Another member of staff was able to act as interpreter for two families. She left a large envelope near the door for parents to return their replies, but was surprised most chose to hand them back to her, as she had handed them out.

Nasra also observed the babies over the coming days. The observations highlighted the concerns of the staff, that the babies now liked crawling on and off their laps at will to explore. She started to collect and clean large cushions and a rug from elsewhere in the nursery, creating a cosy corner with additional soft materials and mobiles. Parents not only responded with written and verbal suggestions but started offering resources and additional funding for a low rocking chair and small settee.

The staff in the baby room felt Nasra had led the project efficiently and supported them in their Key Person roles. Although initially hesitant, Nasra's contingent response had been assertive in offering her help with an identified need and had instigated change.

REFLECTIVE TASK

- *How do you think the two staff members were initially feeling about:*
  - *instigating EYFS in the baby room?*
  - *having Nasra as an EYP Candidate for Validation in their setting?*
- *How do you think Nasra was feeling about having to lead and support practice in an age group she was just becoming familiar with?*
- *What relationship skills did she use to lead and support?*
- *How does this situation relate to your experience?*

Ways to lead and support others within Early Years practice will now be demonstrated using the EYFS Principles into Practice cards for Positive Relationships as a source for discussion.

Respecting each other (2.1)

This card starts with a statement that is central to this book, *Every interaction is **based on caring professional relationships** and respectful acknowledgement of the **feelings** of children and their families.* The bold emphasis is in EYFS (DCSF, 2008b, 2.1). This is a heavy demand on staff, assuming this relates to adult–adult interactions as well as adult–child – i.e. every interaction.

A concern sometimes expressed by practitioners and students in settings is the level of painful gossip about and between staff. Could this, at times, be a reaction to the effort of putting on a *caring, professional relationship* to children and families? Although understandable, it fits uncomfortably with some staff who hear it, as well as those who may be directly hurt by it and limits the *growth-promoting climate* for social and emotional well-being.

This card directly relates the importance of adult–adult relationships to the ability to provide positive relationships between children and adults and, with skilled facilitation, could be used to stimulate discussion within a team. An underlying theme here is having the opportunity to extend the emotional vocabulary of staff, allowing them to express their feelings safely without being 'put down'. Phrasing them as 'I' messages rather than 'You . . .' blame messages can alter the nature of the discussion.

PRACTICAL TASK

Try rephrasing the 'You . . .' blaming message to 'I feel . . . when . . .'. Numbers 1 and 2 have been completed as examples.

1. *'You've left that sink in a mess again . . . that's three nights running. You just expect I'll do it so we won't get told off in the morning.'*

becomes:

'I'm really tired again tonight and I feel really fed up that the sink's still in that state. I'm worried about how we'll use it tomorrow.'

2. *'What do you mean you're not coming in again today? That's no excuse! You think you can just do as you please. You have key children to look after here!'*

becomes:

'I'm sorry you're sick again. Look I am concerned. I'd like to set aside time to meet when you come in.'

3. *'You can't really expect us to take the children outside in this. It's wet AND windy.'*

becomes:

---

4. 'Where were you when it was time to tidy up for lunch? On your mobile again!'

becomes:

- *Collect 'blame' statements you have come across and try to rephrase them, or work with colleagues to do so, respecting confidentiality!*

- *You can also support others by trying to identify their feelings verbally; they will soon let you know if you are wrong or right. 'So you really are feeling frustrated about . . ., exhausted . . ., anxious . . ., uncertain . . .'*

- *Collecting a staff 'feelings vocabulary' may be enlightening! There is appreciation that these skills can be developed over time and the process is not as straightforward as implied on the card. Recognising their own feelings helps everyone to understand other people's feelings and to become more caring towards others (2.1).*

Two of the challenges posed on this Principle into Practice card (2.1) are:

- *Having strong feelings about an issue which may be a barrier to supporting a child or their family if they encounter a similar event or experience.*

- *Having strong relationships in the team which make other team members feel excluded or inadequate so they stop speaking up.*

Strong feelings and relationships can be positive if they encourage support of a child and allow for turn-taking and sharing. An EYP trying to lead and support in such circumstances can provide opportunities to find out what is behind the strong feelings that are creating barriers. At times, a practitioner may not even be aware that their behaviour is a barrier to others or limiting support.

An exercise that can be facilitated within a staff team of four or more allows individuals to experience and practise active listening skills that can also strengthen supportive relationships. The skills can be used to talk through challenges and dilemmas like those above.

Three-way reflective listening and listening for feelings

Try this 'Active Listening' exercise out with a small group or identify the skills within it to recognise facts and feelings. Allow 30 minutes for groups of three.

> *Aim: To identify and practise the skill of reflecting back accurately the person's facts and feelings.*

> *Three people take turns as speaker, listener or observer. The speaker talks for five minutes on a self-chosen topic such as an event, good and bad parts of my day, a relationship or a problem describing it as fully as possible. The three decide who will speak first. One will listen and the third person will observe.*

PRACTICAL TASK *continued*

This activity enables the speaker to hear and consider a reflection of what has been said. The second person can be asked to describe, in three minutes, what the speaker has said. The speaker has a further opportunity to describe how it felt to hear the reflection; was it accurate, surprising, un/comfortable? It is important that the speaker is not persuaded into 'accepting' feelings that were not felt just because the listener identified them.

The observer will note and feed back how the speaker and listener behaved (one minute). Did the speaker look relaxed? Did the listener make good eye contact, encouraging remarks, mirror the speaker's body language? It is important that each person experiences speaking, listening and observing.

(adapted from Rawlings, 1996, page 47)

The exercise draws out key points for active listening.

- *Full attention to verbal and non-verbal behaviour requires listening and observation skills.*

- *It provides an opportunity to express FACTS and FEELINGS.*

- *By separating FACTS from FEELINGS it may be possible to identify triggers for emotions from the facts.*

- *The power of emotions can be appreciated and the person feels heard.*

- *The FACTS can then become the focus for identifying possible 'next step' actions.*

- *TIME has been well-spent!*

- *The more active listening skills are practised and used, the more they become part of daily practice, building positive relationships.*

Parents as Partners (2.2)

Scope for leading and supporting other Early Years practitioners in this field requires you, as an EYP, to first reflect on your own beliefs and attitudes about Parents as Partners. Does this initial statement ring true within personal practice?

> *Parents are children's first and most enduring educators. When **parents and practitioners work together** in Early Years settings, the results have a **positive impact on children's development** and learning.*

(DCSF, 2008b)

There is recognition that *all practitioners will benefit from professional development in diversity, equality and anti-discriminatory practice whatever the ethnic, cultural or social make-up of the setting* (DCSF, 2008b). EYPs can support staff by encouraging them to go on Local Authority, or national, training programmes, and then cascade information to colleagues, continuing to reflect on impact on practice over time. Local Authorities, or settings near you, may have been involved in specific projects such as Margy Whalley's *Parents*

Involved in their Children's Learning (PICL): The Pen Green Framework for Engaging Parents (2007). If so, arrange for other Early Years practitioners or parents to share their experiences with your team. Each Local Authority will also have a support network for EYPs and Candidates on training, so make contact and encourage others to do likewise.

How can you make information relevant and available to colleagues for reading and discussion? Articles, poems and quotes from Foundation Degree programmes have been known to end up displayed in staff toilets! Access to the internet at work can provide links to such resources as the Fatherhood Institute, for Burgess's latest research on *Fathers and Parenting Interventions: What Works?* (2009). Materials on the EYFS CD-ROM (DCSF, 2008) can continue to provide practical suggestions as well as issues for debate. Click on 'Resources and Positive Relationships' and look at the Sure Start Research Reports *Use of Childcare Among Families with Children who have Special Educational Needs* (Bryson *et al.*, 2005) and *Use of Childcare Among Families from Minority Ethnic Backgrounds* (Bell *et al.*, 2005).

REFLECTIVE TASK

Strategies parents use that make them successful educators

Take each of the five numbered strategies below in turn, and reflect on them in relation to:

- *your own attitudes and beliefs about parents as partners;*
- *ways these strategies are evident in your personal practice;*
- *ways these strategies are evident within your setting;*
- *how you may use these strategies to lead and support other Early Years practitioners to build positive relationships.*

1. ***Love and care*** – the bond . . . surfaces under all manner of stresses and strains to reassure the child of the strength of the relationships between them *(Sylva and Lunt, 1982)*.

2. ***Operate in the real world***. Parents talk to their children around the house, in the community and during meals. They are there when the 'why's', 'what's' and 'how's' are asked.

3. *Usually, parents **give time to learn**; time to pose meaningful questions and to come up with their own theories and hypotheses; time to try things out, to make mistakes and to try again, time to leave things be, to return to them at will and to revisit things when the time is right; time to be distracted and to take a detour from their original path or goal and to learn by accident rather than design.*

4. *Often they are in a **1:1 relationship, or very small groups**, when the questions are asked. In the home, children are able to talk about a range of topics, to initiate and sustain conversations and to ask questions endlessly and all of these factors make the home a powerful learning environment (Tizard and Hughes, 1984).*

5. *In these situations parents usually **respond to, rather than initiate learning**. The child wants to know, wants to know what to do, wants to know what to do next – and the parent supplies the answers – supporting and facilitating.*

(adapted from Fisher, 2008, page11)

All the above skills relate to background theories discussed in previous chapters, supporting Gerhardt's *Why Love Matters* (2004), Gopnik's *How Babies Think* (2001), McMullen and Dixon's *Relationship-Based Approach to Early Years Practice* (2009) and Papatheodorou and Moyles' *Relationship Pedagogy* (2009). Sharing material like this to lead and support staff should help Early Years practitioners feel they are directly involved in a reflective learning community with a 'listening culture'. Gradually, relational language develops around the material discussed.

Supporting Learning (2.3)

The relationship skills from the above sections are crucial to support learning (see Chapter 5).

How can you convince others, if they need it, about the difference each member of staff makes, in relation to this statement from the Principles into Practice card 2.3?

> *Warm, **trusting relationships** with knowledgeable adults support children's learning **more effectively than any amount of resources.***

> (DCSF, 2008b)

Staff will support and encourage each other, learning informally or on the periphery, as well as directly. Evidence of ways practitioners verbally and non-verbally motivate each other throughout routines during the day is worth capturing, as Luff found when looking at key ways in which Early Childhood practitioners enable very young children's active, participatory learning (2009, page 129). Her examples of interactions between Early Years practitioners showed how they *operated in a highly professional manner; in their interactions with one another; in the support and recognition they offer to childcare students working in the nursery; and in the ways in which they relate to the children's parents* (Luff, 2009).

CASE STUDY

Legitimate peripheral participation
Mij and Kel are friends but they avoid the temptation to chat socially while they are working with the children. They do share jokes, for example, laughing when Kel changes Jesse and realises what he has been playing with because he has sand in his nappy. There is evidence of their care for one another when Kel returns from lunch complaining that her eyes are itching and Mij sends her to wash them. When Kel is saying goodbye to Mij, as she leaves at the end of her shift, another affectionate incident occurs. As the children join in and wave, Sophie says 'Mij!'. Kel excitedly calls after Mij saying, 'Sophie said your name!' and she encourages Sophie to repeat this new word.

These positive interactions also extend to other colleagues. There is evidence of respect and shared working, including checking with one another before leaving the room for any reason.

This friendly and encouraging attitude is maintained towards students working in the nursery on work placement for their Diploma in Child Care and Education (the same qualification that Kel and Mij recently attained). They are made welcome in the team and are well supported. As a part of their course, they have to complete written observations of the children and both Mij and Kel discuss these with them. Kel talks to one of the students who is uncertain about how she can record Jem's language development, and later in the day invites the students to observe and record as she interacts with him, encouraging him to 'vocalize'. The other student gives Mij a copy of her observation of Jem's motor skills and Mij thanks her, looks at it and recognises its contribution, promising to include the observation in Jem's record folder.

In keeping with a model of situated learning within the workplace (Lave and Wenger, 1991; Wenger, 1998) the students learn by engagement in the social practices of the nursery.

(drawn from Luff, 2009, pages 139,140)

REFLECTIVE TASK

- *How does the experience of Kel and Mij relate to ways you are being supported by colleagues?*

- *Reflect on what you learnt through 'legitimate peripheral participation' as a student in a setting.*

- *How may these influence ways you lead and support others now in building up positive relationships?*

This section recognises the impact of a web-like supportive structure that can develop within a setting, including a childminder's home, as positive relationships are built and maintained by informal as well as formal structures. It is these that help to create the atmosphere children, families, staff and visitors experience on entry, with the potential to encourage positive learning dispositions for all, as already explored in Chapter 5.

Key Person (2.4)

A key person has special responsibilities for working with a small number of children, giving them the reassurance to feel safe and cared for and building relationships with their parents.

(DCSF, 2008b, 2.4).

- There are expectations that *a key person develops a genuine bond with children and offers a settled, close relationship* (2.4). One of the potential challenges or conflicts arising here is how to meet a child's needs for a key person *while being concerned for staff who may feel over-attached to a child* (2.4). Leadership and support may allow time to help individual Early Years practitioners in these roles separate facts from feelings through active listening, as covered earlier. Informed decisions can be made about the quality of interactions within a 'genuine bond' using material from Gerhardt (2004), Gopnik (2001) and Elfer *et al.* (2009). A genuine bond will develop from Rogers' conditions (1995, page 115) for a *growth-promoting climate*:

- *genuineness;*
- *unconditional positive regard;*
- *empathic understanding.*

Inevitably this will share powerful feelings – from happiness to disgust, anger, fear, jealousy or guilt – as the practitioner tunes-in to the baby, toddler or young child. Observation techniques in Early Years have focused on objectivity, highlighting facts at the expense of emotions. As EYFS (2008) is recognising the importance of emotional literacy, value will inevitably be placed also on learning about a young child through positive relationships, sharing emotional ups and downs. The Tavistock Method of Observation, originally grounded in psychotherapy and health models, has been recognised in Early Years with the introduction of *Birth to Three Matters* (DfES, 2002). Here, practitioners are encouraged to write about their observations of a child in narrative form after the event, including emotional experiences for themselves as well as participants. This has clear links to Rogers' *growth-promoting climate* and the relationship-based approach to Early Years practice.

REFLECTIVE TASK

Co-regulation – emotions 'riding in tandem'

Childminders often have more expertise in the experience of genuine bonding over time than some other practitioners, being more likely to stay attached to a child throughout their Early Years and sometimes beyond. Jane Mitchell (2009) has shared her experiences from both childminding and adoption to write about the challenges of empathy and attachment.

She uses the term 'co-regulation' to look at what can be aimed for, and strategies for the child and adult.

Read through excerpts from Jane's article, aimed mainly at adoptive parents as they live with the ups and downs with children who may carry heavy emotional baggage.

How closely are our emotions 'riding in tandem' with our relationships?

Does our stress response move with a child's?

If yes, it is due to bonding/attachment – emotional empathy. We want to match their emotions to help them recognise their ups and downs as we become attuned. We can then recognise when they need space, including a place to be angry, or to have a 'scream'.

'Rupture and repair' helps build up resilience. Mistakes can be worked through with others.

It is useful to match your child's excitement, empathise with their fear, anger or sorrow. If they feel you are attuned to their emotions you will be able to use that connection to regulate them back to a calm state.

REFLECTIVE TASK *continued*

An Adoption UK parent support programme uses a traffic lights approach to help identify your emotional states as well as the child's.

Green	*Calm, relaxed, regulated emotions*
Amber	*Entering a stressed state rather than relaxed – agitated, worried, distracted*
	Less tolerance, 'short fuse'
	Less able to help child regulate their feelings
	Inability to concentrate, hypervigilance, impatient, restless, disturbed sleep
	Scared, defensive behaviour
Red	*Stress overload – anger, fear, sorrow, pain*
	Fuse blows. Loss of control
	Increased heart rate
	Potential to destruct, discharge these emotions!

Strategies to help the practitioner co-regulate children's feelings:

- *Take time to reflect, with help of friend, colleague.*

- *Identify facts that may act as triggers – time of day, part of routine, short-staffed, personality clash, health issues . . .*

- *What message is the child trying to give?*

- *Acknowledge the power of the feelings – anger, helplessness, exhaustion, frustration.*

- *Look for a range of options to try out.*

- *Select one or two small steps to try first, then with others if those do not have an effect in order to 'self-care'.*

(adapted from Mitchell, 2009)

1. *Does the 'traffic light' imagery help identify different emotional states an Early Years practitioner may experience?*

2. *What may trigger children to enter the 'amber' or 'red' zones, and what behaviour may they show?*

3. *An Early Years practitioner can co-regulate amber or red behaviour if they are empathising with a child in their care. How may that present to colleagues?*

4. *What strategies, selected from above, can be used to support a colleague at this time?*

5. *As the practitioner becomes calmer, the child will also co-regulate and show signs of 'calming'. In what ways can the surrounding environment help this?*

6. *How can the strategies that both the child and Early Years practitioner use to move back to amber or green state be owned within the setting?*

'Rupture and repair' builds up resilience is a powerful statement, acknowledging the learning of life skills to use through rough times. This is again 'real world' experience. Can EYPs identify their own strengths and areas for development to support colleagues in these secondary or multiple attachment relationships? The EYFS Principles into Practice cards can, therefore, be used to stimulate discussion and reflection on ways to support practitioners in building positive relationships, while extending ownership of the Principles themselves.

Formal ways to lead and support Early Years practitioners

Each setting will have its own formal structures for induction and staff appraisals. These can include times to offer leadership and support but also include a degree of disciplinary and quality assurance procedures so will not be considered here.

Other specific ways to lead and support Early Years practitioners will just be outlined and considered within the context of a relationship-based approach to practice.

Coaching offers:

- direct support for specific means;

- instruction or demonstration;

- goal setting.

There is a definite place for constructive coaching, especially where the Early Years practitioner or student identifies a need and an EYP or other colleague has the required expertise. It is a matter of making sure the right person is in the right place at the right time with the right knowledge, also able to set the next right goals!

Role-modelling offers:

- a relevant, specific example of how to carry out a task or communicate constructively e.g. *learning dispositions are 'caught not taught'* (anon).

Mediator skills help people to manage conflict for themselves, using active listening skills, a non-judgemental approach and taking responsibility for choosing constructive steps that respect and value others (Rawlings,1996). This approach sits comfortably within a relationship-based approach to practice and benefits from specific training. The skills can be used within daily conflict, but when used to manage a conflict situation it is best if the mediator is 'neutral', outside direct working relationships with the disputants.

A **mentor** can be seen as the 'one in the middle' in Early Years practice (Callan and Copp, 2006, in Fowler *et al.*, 2009, page 17). Different structures of mentoring exist within work-based practice. In Early Years, mentors have been an essential requirement for students on Sector-endorsed Foundation Degrees, the role usually being filled by someone within the workplace or the locality. Currently, mentoring is also offered for Candidates on the EYPS Validation Pathway, with different requirements again for those on the Full Pathway who gain work experience from different settings, to those on routes where their evidence is gathered mainly from within their own role.

Successful mentoring is set within an action-reflection cycle and is based on the key principles of confidentiality, credibility and clarity, and ultimately engenders trust between those involved (Fowler *et al.*, 2009, page 217). Mentoring allows for the development of positive relationship building skills, so can be a direct way to support Early Years practitioners develop these skills. *Positive feelings and responses can be generated by the close relationship that exists* (Fowler *et al.*, 2009, page 221). However, clear boundaries need to be set here, as within any relationship. The term 'professional friend' for mentor is sometimes used, but to maintain trust this needs clarification. There should still be a direct line manager for each practitioner to monitor this 'friendship'.

So, the key ethical principles for mentoring are *confidentiality, credibility and clarity of role . . . all of which engender trust between those involved* (Fowler *et al.*, 2009, page 219). These specific roles may be undertaken by an EYP, and will be considered further in Chapter 7 in regard to CPD.

C H A P T E R   S U M M A R Y

This chapter has identified ways to build trust through supporting staff, in order to strengthen the foundations for positive relationships throughout Early Years practice, remembering the initial quote: *Trust is a peculiar resource; it is built rather than depleted by use.*

The extent of interactions throughout the day between children and adults, including families, shows the impact positive relationships can have in all aspects of Early Years provision. Just looking at the main relevant Standards above is a solemn reminder of the need to support all staff in developing these skills, challenging inappropriate interactions if necessary.

The range of staff experience and qualifications within Early Years provision – from childcare students to managers – benefits from individuals clarifying their own roles. These need to be valued and respected, alongside the varied expertise of Candidates on the different EYPS Validation Pathways. Support is best tailored to the needs of the individual within each situation, being *mindful of the moment* and *respectful*.

A range of strategies has been identified to help an EYP lead and support other Early Years practitioners, including mentoring, and role-modelling.

There have been opportunities to reflect on key issues arising in terms of relational pedagogy and the CPD of the supportive EYP.

Moving On

As in other chapters, reflection has been instrumental in exploring the impact of background theories, knowledge and alternative practice or pedagogy on 'Positive and Trusting Relationships' with children in Early Years Settings. Current research has been identified, already exploring the development of relational pedagogy and a relationship-based approach to practice. The final chapter will consider 'Reflection and Learning' for the EYP within this climate. The potential to work within learning communities, using the skills of a reflective practitioner, will further enhance relationship skills with children, parents and colleagues. Young children can then move forward in their journeys with confidence, curiosity and motivation to keep on learning.

Self-assessment question

Take each point from McMullen and Dixon's (2009, pages 125, 126) suggestions for establishing and maintaining positive relationships within Early Years practice.

Identify an example in this chapter that you can use to help you lead and support another practitioner with this skill.

Be mindful by:

1. *being fully present in the moment with your relationship partner;*

2. *being a responsive communicator, attentive to and aware of the impact of our own and our partners' verbal and non-verbal messages.*

Be reflective by:

3. *being aware of how our own background, beliefs and experiences shape and filter our perceptions of others' behaviours and influence our own responses and behaviours;*

4. *being deliberate in our actions and communications, considering beforehand what we will do and say, paying careful attention to how it is interpreted, and engaging in critical self-assessment following each encounter or behavioural episode.*

Be respectful by:

5. *valuing and honouring the differences in our relationship partners, and treating them all as competent and worthwhile;*

6. *being more holistic in our thinking and engaging in 'both/and' ways of approaching issues and problems rather than one more dualistic 'either/or' or 'right/wrong' thinking.*

FURTHER READING

Fowler, K, Robins, A, Callan, S and Copp, E (2009) Fostering Identity and Relationships: The Essential Role of Mentors in Early Childhood, in Papatheodorou, T and Moyles, J, *Learning Together in the Early Years: Exploring Relational Pedagogy.* London: Routledge.

Insley, S and Lucas, K (2009) Making the Most of the Relationship Between Two Adults to Impact on Early Childhood Pedagogy, in Papatheodorou, T and Moyles, J, *Learning Together in the Early Years: Exploring Relational Pedagogy.* London: Routledge.

Luff, P (2009) Looking and Listening for Participatory Practice in an English Day Nursery, in Berthelsen, D, Brownlee, J and Johansson, E (eds.) *Participatory Learning in the Early Years: Research and Pedagogy.* London: Routledge.

7 Reflection and learning as an Early Years Professional

Well-placed trust grows out of active inquiry rather than blind acceptance.

(O'Neill, 2002, page 76)

CHAPTER OBJECTIVES

Reflective practice is one of the two main attributes that distinguish the professionalism of EYPs who have gained EYPS. The second is the ability to lead and support colleagues in order to effect change and improve outcomes for children (CWDC, 2008, page 5). EYPs each need the positive learning dispositions discussed in Chapter 5 for the children, including motivation, curiosity, reflection, perseverance, confidence, courage, trust and playfulness.

This chapter will draw together the international background theories that underpin the reflective nature of a relationship-based approach to practice. The Reflective Learning Cycle approach (Pollard, 2005, page 17) to implementing change will be discussed in terms of relational issues, including children as co-researchers. The development of 'reflective learning communities' of EYPs will be explored, acknowledging a process of active inquiry for Early Years practice.

Key theories, reflective and practical tasks, and a case study will link to the following EYPS Standards:

S24: Be accountable for the delivery of high quality provision.

S25: Establish fair, respectful, trusting, supportive and constructive relationships with children.

S33: Establish and sustain a culture of collaborative working between colleagues.

S38: Reflect on and evaluate the impact of practice, modifying approaches where necessary, and take responsibility for identifying and meeting their professional development needs.

S39: Take a creative and constructively critical approach towards innovation, and adapt practice if benefits and improvements are identified.

After reading this chapter you should be able to:

- select national and international background theories that inform and inspire your practice and encourage you to 'have-a-go' at implementing change;

- identify ways to use and share specific skills and resources for reflective practice with colleagues, children and families, enabling collaboration;

- own and adapt, as necessary, the Reflective Learning Cycle;

- explore opportunities to join or develop a 'reflective learning community';

- claim your identity as an EYP who is a reflective practitioner.

Introduction: Early Years Professionals as reflective practitioners

EYPs are pioneers, developing quality provision for 0–5 year olds in homes, pre-schools, full daycare settings, nurseries and nursery schools, crèches, Children's Centres and beyond. The last ten years have seen the EYFS emerge out of the *Curriculum Guidance for the Foundation Stage* (DfEE, 2000) and *Birth to Three Matters* (DfES, 2002) and underpinned by the Every Child Matters agenda (DfES, 2003). Childcare legislation has placed Early Years within the Children's Workforce (0–19 years) with a move towards inter-professional working. How can you claim the identity of the EYP within this inter-professional field? – more relationships! Parents – mothers and fathers – are justifiably acknowledged as partners but, on many occasions, pay for childcare and staff salaries, so quality provision will be measured economically. The development of Children's Centres has placed the focus on holistic learning and development of children within the local community, drawing on Bronfenbrenner's 'ecological model' (1979). The EYP has to engage with the local community, acknowledging cultural and environmental needs that impact on outcomes for children. This picture will always just be a snapshot, due to the pace and enormity of change.

It is precisely within this picture that the reflective skills and wisdom of an EYP is crucial. Eighteen of the 39 Standards for EYPs centre around effective practice with children. Knowledge of effectiveness comes within positive relationships – observation, accurate recording and awareness of feelings as well as facts, responsive planning, shared discussion with children, parents and colleagues and honest critical evaluation. The importance of specific communication skills to deliver effective practice has been highlighted in previous chapters. The EYP is in a position to reflect on delivery of practice in light of the changing national and international scene and new knowledge arising from research. This can be a heady cocktail, as students on Sector-Endorsed Foundation Degree Early Years and BA (Hons) Early Years courses find, as they often combine full-time employment with study. However, one advantage of this type of programme has been sharing experiences with practitioners across a range of provision and from diverse backgrounds. Relationship

---

REFLECTIVE TASK

Relationship skills and reflective practice
Think back over projects, including specific research, carried out during degree programmes, whatever the subject.

Look back at skills covered in previous chapters as needed.

What skills have you developed in regard to working with others to help you in ongoing reflective practice?

What specific communication skills have you used to acquire evidence?

What positive learning dispositions have you developed (Chapter 5)?

Once EYPS is gained, these skills of reflective practice need to become embedded into Early Years provision.

skills emerge through delivering presentations, researching in small groups and sharing the struggles of tight time management. A similar experience occurs with EYP Candidates on other Pathways who are able to appreciate the range of background expertise of their peers and develop respectful collaborative skills.

Reflective practice

Work-based learning depends on relationships, as demonstrated by Rawlings (2008, page 23) in a Key Components Framework: Early Years work-based study. Here, the central strand, roles, responsibilities and relationships, has links on either side to *theory, knowledge, skills and understanding* and *application in the workplace*. An EYP, as said before, is work-based and has theory, knowledge and understanding of Early Years and so will continually have to update in both these areas. What is crucial is that the relationship strand is also refreshed in order to maximise the link between the others. This includes self-awareness and self-motivation, which are essential as the level of autonomy/independence may well increase.

PRACTICAL TASK

Identifying relationship abilities for reflective practice

Examine each of the specific reflective practitioner skills below, drawn from Rawlings (2008, page 23), and consider how you will find opportunities to use and develop them.

Relationship abilities – self and others

- *Knowledge of self and others.*
- *Personal philosophies.*
- *Management of self and working with others.*
- *Knowledge and understanding of the child.*
- *Use of technology, including internet, email and mobile phone communication.*
- *Developing research questions.*
- *Conflict management strategies and skills.*
- *Recognising one's own strengths and areas for development.*
- *Self-evaluation.*
- *Taking courage to question your certainties (Malaguzzi, 1993).*
- *Ability to value self and others.*
- *Managing change.*
- *Empathy.*
- *Ability to listen.*
- *Effective communication.*

PRACTICAL TASK continued

- *Ability to collaborate and problem solve.*

- *Equal opportunities.*

- *Ability to see and recognise one's own and others' triggers for powerful feelings.*

- *Study.*

- *Time management.*

- *Curiosity, motivation and creativity.*

- *Work, rest and time to relax!*

Select three relationship abilities that you wish to develop further.

For each one, identify a 'next step' to enable you to develop that ability.

Keeping the professionalism in reflection and learning

Carrying out reflective practice as part of a qualification course satisfies assessment procedures at that specific level of academic achievement, whether 5, 6 or beyond to Masters programmes. The EYP has to, then, be intrinsically motivated to keep learning. The dynamics arising within relationships in the setting are always a sound place to start. As explored in Chapter 6, Early Years practitioners are most likely to benefit from support if it ties in with where they are. In the same way, an EYP is most likely to engage constructively to bring about change in areas of interest and direct involvement.

Professionalism in learning comes from continually being curious and searching out information, whether through attending training, reading – including surfing the net – or sharing with colleagues. Internationally, the Early Years scene is a rich source of inspiration and evidence to inform potential changes in practice. Think back to practice in other countries which has impacted on your understanding of the changing roles and relationships within Early Years. Malaguzzi's philosophy (Edwards *et al.*, 1998) behind the development of the Reggio Emilia nurseries in Italy may already have filtered through to the way you set up your learning environment, organise projects or document children's work. The family and community involvement in New Zealand's 'Te Whariki', with its holistic approach to Early Years education, has influenced the development of EYFS (DCSF, 2008) and hence all our practice. The Forest Schools of Scandinavia have led to adaptations in practice to celebrate outdoor learning experiences in communities in England and Scotland. The strong live music and story-telling traditions of the West Indies and Africa has rejuvenated willingness amongst some practitioners to 'have-a-go', learning from others. Meditation and other spiritual prayer and listening exercises from Asia and the East are filtering in to Early Years – a reminder of the spiritual self and the value of quiet reflection. These changes depend on reflective practitioners valuing the settings they are in, while looking at ways to use new knowledge and engage in the 'real world' of their local community.

Claiming your identity as an EYP

Personalise CWDC's wording in a job description for an EYP below to include your specific abilities as a reflective practitioner. You may know what you are capable of, but many others will not. Identify what you do, and so what you may expect other EYPs to do.

An EYP generic job description

A job description fits your specific needs. CWDC will not write this for you, but here is some information that may come in useful when outlining your requirements:

It is important to draw a distinction between leading practice and managing a setting. Although the same person can sometimes hold both roles, an EYP is trained to lead practice. This involves the following:

- *Possessing the highest standards and latest knowledge of practice and serving as an example to the other practitioners within the settings.*

- *Providing advice to other practitioners with practice-related issues. This could include one-to-one coaching, as well as group sessions. Other support could involve planning an experience or reflecting on an activity.*

(www.cwdcouncil.org/eyps/employers/faqs)

Remember that your 'highest standards' and 'latest knowledge of practice' will feed in to your reflections. You are then in a position to share sound evidence with others.

Read Nurse's definition of Early Years Professional for her book title *The New Early Years Professional: Dilemmas and Debates* (2007):

> 'Professional' in our title takes on the meaning of all those who work with young children and their families, who have some training and expertise, but with differing qualifications and experience. This is an 'inclusive' model of a 'profession', rather than the 'exclusive' view held traditionally.

(Nurse, 2007, pages 3, 4)

How do you then respectfully respond to other Early Years practitioners who justifiably say they are acting as professionals? An example of the difficulties here was expressed by one of the first childminders in the country to acquire EYPS. She soon stopped sharing this information with other childminders as the news was received with hostility. Others felt they offered a quality service and parents certainly would not pay more. As well as childminding, this EYP acted on her own reflections and has started to deliver some training at a local college, using her leading and supporting skills too. What is important is that each individual finds clarity and self-respect in recognition of their own role.

Reflective practice in action

So, how will you, as an EYP, demonstrate reflective practice and learning in terms of positive relationships? The positive learning dispositions mentioned at the start may provide a clue – motivation, curiosity, reflection, perseverance, confidence, courage, trust and play-fulness. These tie in with the earlier practical and reflective tasks and directly relate to relationships with children, colleagues and families.

What happens when these learning dispositions are in use? The following case study is a write-up, by an EYP, Becky, for the Parent Noticeboard at a day nursery of the 'sponta-neous' progression of an activity to suit the particular dynamics of this group.

Each numbered statement was accompanied by a photo of that stage (unable to be included).

CASE STUDY

The nursery celebrates 'Fish Day'

Yesterday we ate fish pasta for lunch; some of the pre-schoolers started to discuss what fish they were eating and where it might have come from.

1. *Luckily Becky went 'fishing' last night at the fishmongers.*

2. *Becky caught a 'BIG' mackerel.*

3. *We wanted to find out what was inside the mackerel, so we cut it open.*

4. *Like us it had intestines, two eyes, a mouth and sharp teeth.*

5. *It also had scales.*

6. *We chopped the head off to see its mouth and gills.*

7. *It felt very slippery and slimy.*

8. *J. told the (other) children that 'we don't have gills to breathe'.*

9. *Inside the mackerel we found a 'back bone'. S. told us 'If it didn't have a back bone it would be all floppy'.*

10. *The outside of the fish felt very smooth and cold.*

11. *The back bone was spiky and hard.*

12. *The children wanted to take a closer look at the fish's eye.*

13. *D. found the 'swim bladder'. This helps the fish to swim the right way up!*

14. *After, we wiped our hands before . . .*

15. *Giving them a good scrub in the bathroom.*

16. *We showed the toddlers what remained of the mackerel.*

We also had a brief chat about 'heaven' and discussed how the fish could be dead, but not up in heaven. Becky explained that fish have a soul, which is like a 'little bit of magic'. When the fish was caught the soul went to heaven but the fish's body stayed behind so we could eat it. As the children left the pre-school room, completely unprompted they said 'Sorry fish' and then asked when they could eat it!

---

17. *D., the cook, prepared the mackerel for our snack.*

18. *Here she is putting it in the oven (I did catch two fish Mummies and Daddies – we're **not** eating the one we investigated).*

19. *Here we are eating the mackerel, it was deeeeeeeelicious!*

    P.S. For Daddies day the pre-schoolers would like to take their daddies fishing! Enjoy!

REFLECTIVE TASK

- *How do you feel when reading the documentation, bearing in mind much of the sensory experience will be hard to re-capture?*

- *What relationship skills are present?*

- *What reflective skills are shown by the children and Becky?*

- *What emotions appear to be present in Becky and the children?*

The reflective learning cycle

There are variations on a reflective learning cycle, but a key fact is the continuity, with one stage leading into another, sometimes seamlessly and at others with careful consideration.

The case study above will now be linked to a reflective learning cycle; see if you agree with the connections.

1. Becky and the children were discussing and **reflecting** on what fish were in the pasta they were eating.

2. Becky continued to **reflect** and then **planned.**

3. She **made provision** by visiting the fishmonger that night, buying mackerel, preparing other staff, including the cook, and finding a sharp knife and chopping board. She also spoke to parents to share what she intended to do, asked another member of staff to support her and take photos as documentation and checked the children's allergy list.

4. Becky, colleagues and the children **acted** out the plan.

5. **Evidence was collected** in narrative and photographic form.

6. The evidence was **analysed** by Becky, other staff, parents and children.

7. **Evaluation of evidence** occurred alongside the analysis as discussion took place. Even the fishmonger gave a reaction when more mackerel were later bought to demonstrate the activity to an EYP Support Network group. Feedback from this group of EYPs provided additional critical evaluation of the activity and recognition of the intense learning opportunity for all. Constructive criticism included consideration of potential gender stereotyping.

8. Further **reflection** by children and adults led to identification of next steps, including a potential fishing trip for fathers, suggested by the children!

This process has covered all the stages of the reflective learning cycle (Pollard, 2005, page 17), starting with listening to the voices of the children and also bringing in an additional dimension of an EYP Support Network.

A reflective learning community

As stated at the beginning of the chapter, the Early Years scene continues to change and as an EYP you are in position to identify the impact EYPs can have on quality provision. CWDC has provided, for these first few years, funding support to Local Authorities to establish Early Years Professional Support Networks (CWDC, 2009). These operate in different ways to address local needs, but usually offer specific training sessions and chances for EYPs to share effective practice. They provide opportunities for 'dialogue' arising from issues in practice.

Evidence is already available from Reggio Emilia of how Early Years staff come together to share documentation and plan (Edwards *et al.*, 1998). Dahlberg also talks about adapting these patterns and finding ways for practitioners to join up from different settings.

> *Change needs networking combined with documentation (. . . from pedagogical practice . . .) and reflection. You need to start with a view, a construction which sees children as rich and competent, and from the work of the children and not the conditions of the pedagogues.*

> (Dahlberg, G, 2007, Stockholm Project)

The 'Fish Day' certainly seemed to start with a 'rich' view of children as competent. The dialogue of the children amazed others, supporting Dahlberg's experience. Becky, as a member of an EYP Support Network, showed others the display and gave them a chance to dissect and eat mackerel. Candidates on pathways to EYPS Validation met with established EYPs. There was certainly a sense that *Contradictions (the collision of new and old ideas) are the catalyst for change* (Activity Theory, Engeström, 2000, 2001). Evidence of learning from use of sustained, shared thinking in the children's discussion with Becky was as much an area for reflection for all as gutting the mackerel with a very sharp knife!

A chance to meet in this way as reflective practitioners builds on the work of Wenger, who recognises *a community of practice is a place for the acquisition of knowledge, for example from colleagues, but can also become 'a locus for the creation of knowledge'* (Wenger, 1998, page 86). Wenger's study of patterns of learning within social interactions led to the development of the idea of *communities of practice* (Wenger, 1998, page 86).

In relation to the EYP Support Networks, each EYP is engaged in their own practice, although guided by the EYFS. Further exploration into Wenger's work may acknowledge his recognition of two processes that complement each other in the creation of new knowledge.

- 'Participation' as the individuals come together and share knowledge and experience, enhancing the overall content of their meeting.

- 'Reification' – where this new knowledge becomes more concrete in the form of text, policies and procedures and changes on practice. This process may become more visible in Early Years practice, as research documentation of the impact of change is produced by EYPs themselves.

These two processes acknowledge a community of practice, or reflective learning community, as allowing for *shared histories of learning* (Wenger, 1998, page 86). Relationship skills remain central. Within such a group, potential ideas can be shared, arising from current research in a wider field yet directly implemented in individual practice.

Use of co-construction in meaning-making

The ability to compare and contrast are skills that support reflective practice.

Read through Payler's (2009) research around 'co-construction' below and reflect on her questions.

'Co-construction' is a shared space in which the adult and child both have a constructive role to play. Part of the adult's role is to ascertain, suggest or jointly create a goal with the child. Co-construction was found to be more empowering for children and that they engaged in higher order thinking through their involvement *than when the adults scaffolded learning for them (Jordan, in Payler, 2009, page 121).*

Payler's questions arise from a qualitative research study of learning processes among ten four-year-old children in a community-run pre-school and a primary school reception class in the south of England. The preschool had an invisible pedagogy, emphasising social development *and the reception class had* a visible pedagogy, emphasising specific learning outcomes (Payler, 2009, page 120).

The care and socialisation-oriented *preschool fostered* co-construction *between staff and children. Also, where pre-determined learning outcomes were set, collaboration meant active participation from the children. This encouraged risk-taking and allowance of* peripheral participation *to strengthen learner identities. It is* suggested that children from co-constructive backgrounds were able to negotiate the controlled discourse of the reception classroom in a more positive manner (*Payler, 2009, page 135*).

The 'educational-outcomes-oriented' reception class used scaffolding towards predetermined learning objectives. This approach seemed to lead to some direct identification of children as less able, which could impact on their learner identities.

Payler recommends that EYPs reflect on the following in relation to their current practice.

1. *How the ethos and organisation of their settings may be influencing children's meaning-making.*

2. *The guidance strategies the adults routinely use and why.*

3. *Whether/how their guidance strategies are influenced by the ethos of the setting and the implications of this for their own practice.*

4. *Whether their guidance strategies differ for different (groups of) children and how they align to expectations and perceptions of 'ability'.*

5. *The impact of their guidance strategies upon children's possible participation and developing learner identities.*

An interesting point to note is the type of questions Payler uses for reflection. They are similar to the open-ended questions in Chapter 5 suggested for children – 'How?' 'Why?' 'What may be the impact?'

While on Pathways to EYPS Validation, Candidates value opportunities to compare and contrast pedagogy in different settings. The Early Years Professional Support Networks aim to provide opportunities to use these academic skills to raise quality in provision. New terminology is focusing on the importance of the quality of interactions to stimulate learning (see Chapter 5), such as 'sustained, shared thinking'. Can you, as an EYP, help others to make informed, ethical decisions to change?

Ethics within reflective practice

Fair, respectful, trusting, supportive and constructive relationships are only obtained through thoughtful, ethical consideration. Values and beliefs of individuals and groups are then consciously respected.

Current debates around the *ethics of an encounter,* discussed by Dahlberg and Moss (2005), may influence the development of a 'listening culture' within Early Years. The Young Children's Voices Network is currently sharing resources to support *Listening as a Way of Life* (NCB, 2009), as mentioned in Chapter 4.

Rowson's (2006) *Framework for Ethical Thinking in the Professions* can be used by EYPs to engage in decision-making in a way that is consistent with colleagues from health and social care. The FAIR model looks at how issues or problems can be negotiated using values that demonstrate **Fairness** to all parties, allow for the **Autonomy** of individuals and respect the **Integrity** of each in order to seek **Results** that cause the best outcome with minimal harm to all (Rowson, 2009). The use of such a framework, with four key areas, can help individuals and groups to make ethical, informed choices that respect relationships. However, as an EYP, you have to pay specific attention to the children's voice, seeing they are respected in accord with Article 29, UNCRC,1989.

Governments agree that the aim of education must help the fullest possible growth of the child's or young person's personality, talents and mental and physical ability.

Education must help children and young people:

Respect human rights;

Respect their parents;

Respect their and others' culture, language and values;

Have self-respect;

Respect the environment.

(Children's Rights Alliance for England www.crae.org.uk/rights/uncrc.html, accessed 5 January 2010)

REFLECTIVE TASK

The children's voice

- *Look back at the case study above: The nursery celebrates 'Fish Day'.*

- *How were the children 'heard'?*

- *What examples do you have of listening to children within your own reflective practice?*

- *What challenges do you have to address?*

Potential topics for reflective practice

What do you usually reflect on? Questions that take our time and catch our attention usually come from personal interest or in response to a concern that won't go away.

Some of the topics in this book, which generate questions for further exploration, include the following:

- Mother and father partnerships with staff in Early Years settings.

- Key Person approach, acknowledging *the ability to be involved in an intense relationship without being overwhelmed by it* (Elfer *et al.* 2009, page 5).

- Mentoring within Early Years, recognising that *'reflective' practitioners are supported by 'reflective' mentors* and *the guidance offered by the mentor is carried out in the spirit of mutual respect, where power is shared as far as the situation allows, and there is an expectation of two-way learning* (Fowler *et al.* 2009, pages 217, 218).

- Trusting relationships and risk-taking in play (DCSF, 2008, page 08).

PRACTICAL TASK

Future areas for reflection

- *Be 'mindful of the moment' and identify a personal area of interest or concern, or look at the list above of potential areas for development.*

- *Select **one** area that interests you. Write a paragraph about your reasons for the selection, sharing feelings as well as facts.*

- *Identify **one** small next step you can do, generating action from this reflection.*

Reflection as part of a relationship-based approach to Early Years practice

EYPS Standards 38 and 39 acknowledge the skills and abilities used within a reflective planning cycle, continually striving for delivery of high quality provision (S24). Can the respectful nature of a *culture of collaborative working* (S33) with children, colleagues, families and adults lead to empowerment for all? Within this will be appreciation of the *contingent responses* to immediate needs of all involved, present in an ethics of care.

These are examples of the three types of practice drawn together in McMullen and Dixon's (2009) model for a relationship-based approach to practice (Chapter 1 and subsequently).

- 'Mindful' recognises the need for EYPs to be 'in the moment', alert and aware of the needs of the babies and young children.

- 'Respectful' requires recognition and attempts at understanding different values and beliefs of others, bringing this knowledge into the development of positive relationships.

- 'Reflective' acknowledges the EYP's ability to see the reflective practitioner cycle of planning, implementation, evaluation and reflection as also a key process for developing relationships.

Active learning is happening for all, recognising the importance of the ability to 'tune-in' to each other, respect self and others, establish boundaries, and support learning for children and practitioners. This 'learning together' fits the definition of relational pedagogy. *There is a direct correlation between relational pedagogy, sensitivity of carers and the developmental potential of young children* (Dinneen, 2009, page 182).

An invitation from Moyles and Papatheodorou (2009, page 228) in their endpiece on relational pedagogy, is *to begin an exploration of your own understandings, interpretations and practices in order to familiarise yourselves with this important way of thinking, working and learning in early childhood education and care.* As an EYP can you respond to the invitation and use your skills of reflection, learning and ability to establish and sustain positive and trusting relationships?

Trust . . . grows with each successive encounter (Seldon, 2009b, page 191).

C H A P T E R   S U M M A R Y

The focus on reflection and ongoing learning in this chapter highlights the dynamic nature of all the material in a book entitled *Positive and Trusting Relationships in Early Years Settings.* What can be shared in black and white on a written page can only ever attempt to spotlight some of the numerous, rich, multi-sensory encounters within the lives of babies, toddlers, young children, parents and Early Years practitioners, as they come together in Early Years settings. As an EYP, these are the experiences that surely justify a 'relationship-based approach to practice' and the need to 'learn together', as in 'relational pedagogy'. Children and adults can model the positive learning dispositions of motivation, curiosity, reflection, perseverance, confidence, courage, trust and playfulness.

The challenge, now, is to tune-in to those around us, respect others and ourselves, create realistic professional boundaries, lead and support others and keep growing through reflection and learning!

Moving on

2009 saw the publication of two main texts with current research material relevant to *Positive and Trusting Relationships in Early Years Settings*. From the USA came Berthelsen *et al.* (2009) *Participatory Learning in the Early Years: Research and Pedagogy* and from England, Papatheodorou and Moyles (2009) *Learning Together in the Early Years: Exploring Relational Pedagogy*. Both include international perspectives, providing sources for further discussion and potential ongoing research. Are you, as an EYP, keen to continue your studies within a Masters programme? This is certainly a currently active field of inquiry in Early Years practice.

Trust was a national topical issue for 2009, resulting in author Anthony Seldon (2009b) suggesting the idea of a *trust footprint* to rebuild trust within communities. *Every individual and community has a responsibility, year on year, to ensure that the total quantity of trust they generate has increased. An action which damages trust has to be balanced by actions which promote trust and trusteeship for the future to an equal degree* (Seldon, 2009b, page 188). Can we, individually, or as a group, lay down 'trust footprints'?

Self-assessment question

The paragraph below justifies the discovery of 'developmental cognitive science', concerning how much babies and young children in the United States can do, linked to 'nature being nurture'.

When we take care of children, we are also helping the human species find the truth and understand the world. Of course a lot of it is changing diapers and wiping noses and making peanut-butter sandwiches. And a lot of it is worry and exhaustion. But a lot of it, and a lot of the very best of it, the kisses and the pet names, the games and the jokes, turns out to be part of this larger enterprise. We might not have thought that flirting with babies helped solve the Other Minds problem, or that playing hide-and-seek had anything to do with metaphysics, or that baby-talk held the answer to the problem of meaning. But that's just what developmental cognitive science has discovered. We human beings seem designed to complete our grandest projects by pursuing ordinary little joys

(Gopnik *et al.*, 2001, page 211).

Re-write the paragraph for yourself on behalf of EYPs.

Draw on reflections and learning from this book about the effort required, alongside the benefits, of establishing *fair, respectful, trusting, supportive and constructive relationships with children* (S25).

'When we take care of children, we. . . . .'

**FURTHER
READING**

Berthelsen, D, Brownlee, J and Johansson, E (eds.) (2009) *Participatory Learning in the Early Years: Research and Pedagogy.* London: Routledge.

Dineen, F (2009) Relationship Training for Care-Givers in Papatheodorou, T and Moyles, J *Learning Together in the Early Years: Exploring Relational Pedagogy.* London: Routledge.

Seldon, A (2009b) *Trust. How We Lost It and How to Get It Back.* London: Biteback.

References

Amini, F, Lewis, T and Lannon, R (2000) *A General Theory of Love.* New York: Random House.

Association of Professionals in Education and Children's Trusts (ASPECT) www.aspect.org.uk/support/ accessed 6 January 2010.

Association of Teachers and Lecturers. The Education Union www.atl.org.uk/ accessed 24 May 2010.

Badman, G (2009) *Baby Peter Serious Case Review Executive Summary Statement* www.haringeylscb.org/index/news/babypeter_scr.htm accessed 24 May 2010.

Bandura, A (1977) *Social Learning Theory.* Englewood Cliffs, NJ: Prentice Hall.

Barnes, P (ed.) (1995) *Personal, Social and Emotional Development of Children.* Oxford: The Open University. Blackwell.

Bateson, M C (1979) The Epigenesis of Conversational Interaction: A Personal Account of Research Development, in Bulkowa, M (ed.) *Before Speech: The Beginning of Human Communication.* London: Cambridge University Press, pp63–77.

Baumrind, D (1973) The Development of Uninstrumental Competence through Socialization, in Pick, A D (ed.) *Minnesota Symposium on Child Psychology*, 4, Minneapolis: University of Minnesota Press, pp3–46.

Bell, A, Bryson, C, Barnes, M and O'Shea, R (2005) *Use of Childcare among Families from Minority Ethnic Backgrounds.* Nottingham: DfES Publications.

Berthelsen, D, Brownlee, J and Johansson, E (eds.) (2009) *Participatory Learning in the Early Years: Research and Pedagogy.* London: Routledge.

Blandford, S and Knowles, C (2009) *Developing Professional Practice 0–7.* Harlow: Pearson Education Limited.

Boeree, C G (2006) *Personality Theories – Abraham Maslow.* webspace.ship.edu/cgboer/maslow.html. accessed 29 November 2009.

Bowlby, J (1999) *Attachment. Attachment and Loss Vol.1 – 2nd edition.* New York: Basic Books.

Bowlby, R (2009) *Attachment Theory – An Educational DVD.* R Bowlby.

Bronfenbrenner, U (1979) *The Ecology of Human Development: Experiments by Nature and Design.* Cambridge, MA: Harvard University Press.

Brooker, L (2009) 'Just Like Having a Best Friend': How Babies and Toddlers Construct Relationships with their Key Workers in Nurseries, in Papatheodorou, T and Moyles, J (eds.) *Learning Together in the Early Years: Exploring Relational Pedagogy.* London: Routledge.

Brown, B (2001) *Combating Discrimination: Persona Dolls in Action.* Stoke-on-Trent: Trentham Books Ltd.

Brown, B (2008) *Equality in Action. A Way Forward with Persona Dolls.* Trentham Books Ltd.

Bruce, T and Meggitt, C (2006) *Child Care & Education* (4th ed.) London: Hodder Arnold.

Bruner, J and Haste, H (eds.) (1987) *Making Sense. The Child's Construction of the World.* London: Methuen.

Bryson, C, La Valle, I, O'Shea, R and Barnes, M (2005) *Use of Childcare Among Families with Children who have Special Educational Needs.* Nottingham: DfES Publications.

Burgess, A (2009) *Fathers and Parenting Interventions: What Works?* Fatherhood Institute.

Callan, S and Copp, E (2006) The Mentor as the One in the Middle, in Robins, A (ed.) *Mentoring in the Early Years.* London: Sage.

Carr, M and Claxton, G (2004) A Framework for Teaching and Learning. *Early Years:* Vol. 24, No. 1, March 2004.

The Centre for Social Justice (2008) *The Next Generation. A Policy Report from the Early Years Commission.* London: The Centre for Social Justice.

Children's Rights Alliance for England (2009) *UN Convention on the Rights of the Child.* CRAE. www.crae.org.uk/rights/uncrc.html accessed 5 January 2010.

Collins, J (2008) Developing Positive Relationships, in Foley, P, and Leverett, S, *Connecting with Children: Developing Working Relationships.* Bristol: The Policy Press. The Open University.

Cooley, C H (1902) *Human Nature and the Social Order.* New York: Scribner's on www.cf.ac.uk/socsi/undergraduate/introsoc/lkglsslf.html accessed 25 November 2009.

CWDC (Children's Workforce Development Council) (2008) *Guidance to the Standards for the Award of Early Years Professional Status.* Leeds: CWDC.

CWDC (2008) *One Children's Workforce Framework.* CWDC.

CWDC (2009) *Early Years Professional Support Package.* Leeds: CWDC.

Dahlberg, G and Moss, P (2005) *Ethics and Politics in Early Childhood Education.* London: Routledge Falmer.

Dahlberg, G, Moss, P and Pence, A (2007) *Beyond Quality in Early Childhood Education and Care: Languages of Evaluation* (2nd ed.). London: Routledge Falmer.

H.M. Government (1998) *Data Protection Act.* London: HMSO.

Davidson, R J and Irwin, W (1999) The Functional Neuroanatomy of Emotion and Affective Style. *Trends in Neuroscience,* 3: 11–21.

Department for Children, Schools and Families (DCSF) (2007) *The Common Assessment Framework for Children and Young People – A Guide for Practitioners.* Nottingham: DCSF.

Department for Children, Schools and Families (DCSF) (2008a) *Practice Guidance for the Early Years Foundation Stage.* Nottingham: DCSF.

Department for Children, Schools and Families (DCSF) (2008b) *Principles into Practice Cards. The Early Years Foundation Stage.* Nottingham: DCSF.

Department for Children, Schools and Families (DCSF) (2008c) *Statutory Framework for the Early Years Foundation Stage.* Nottingham: DCSF.

Department for Education and Employment (DfEE) (2000) *Curriculum Guidance for the Foundation Stage.* London: Qualifications and Curriculum Authority.

Department for Education and Skills (DfES) (2002) *Birth to Three Matters: A Framework for Supporting Children in Their Earliest Years.* London: DfES.

Department for Education and Skills (DfES) (2003) *Every Child Matters* (Green Paper). London: HMSO. www.dcsf.gov.uk/childrensplan/downloads/ECM%20outcomes%20framework.pdf accessed 20 July 2009.

Department for Education and Skills (DfES) (2005) *Common Core of Skills and Knowledge for the Children's Workforce.* Nottingham: DfES. www.everychildmatters.gov.uk/deliveringservices/commoncore accessed 24 May 2010.

Dineen, F (2009) Relationship Training for Care-Givers, in Papatheodorou, T and Moyles, J *Learning Together in the Early Years: Exploring Relational Pedagogy.* London: Routledge.

Doherty, J and Hughes, M (2009) *Child Development. Theory and Practice 0 –11 Years.* London: Pearson Longman.

Dowling, M (2005) *Young Children's Personal, Social and Emotional Development* (2nd ed.) London: Sage.

Duffy, A, Chambers, F, Croughan, S and Stephens, J (2006) *Working with Babies and Children under Three.* Oxford: Heinemann.

Dunn, J (1988) *The Beginnings of Social Understanding.* Oxford: Blackwell.

Early Childhood Unit (2009) *Listening as a Way of Life. Developing a Listening Culture.* London: National Children's Bureau.

Edwards, C P, Gandini, L and Forman, G (eds.) (1998) *The Hundred Languages of Children: the Reggio Emilia Approach – Advanced Reflections.* London: JAI Press.

Elfer, P, Goldschmeid, E and Selleck, D (2009) *Key Persons in the Nursery. Building Relationships for Quality Provision.* Oxford: David Fulton Publishers.

Engeström,Y (2001) Expansive Learning at Work: Toward an Activity Theoretical Reconceptualisation. *Journal of Education and Work,* Vol. 14, No.1: 133–156.

Erikson, E (1950) *Childhood and Society.* London: Penguin.

Erikson, E (1968) *Identity, Youth and Crisis.* London: Faber.

Erikson, E (1994) *Identity, Youth and Crisis.* London: WW Norton.

Espinosa, L (2009) Set the Stage for Literacy — Literally. A Trusting Relationship and Plenty of Playtime Lay the Foundation for Successful Readers, in *Parent and Child,* Scholastic www2.scholastic.com/browse/article.jsp?id=517&print=1 accessed 3 September 2009.

Fatherhood Institute (2009) *The Big Debate* www.fatherhoodinstitute.org/index.php?id=3&cID=930 accessed 24 May 2010.

Fineman, S (2003) *Understanding Emotion at Work.* London: Sage.

Fisher, J (2008) *Starting from the Child* (3rd ed.) Maidenhead: Open University Press McGraw-Hill Education.

Fogel, A (1993) *Developing through Relationships: Origins of Communication, Self and Culture.* Chicago, IL: University of Chicago Press.

Fowler, K, Robins, A, Callan, S and Copp, E (2009) Fostering Identity and Relationships. The Essential

Role of Mentors in Early Childhood, in Papatheodorou, T and Moyles, J *Learning Together in the Early Years: Exploring Relational Pedagogy.* London: Routledge.

Garner, R (2009) Infant School Exclusions are Rising, Study Shows *The Independent,* 31 December 2009, page 16.

Gerhardt, S (2004) *Why Love Matters – How Affection Shapes a Baby's Brain.* London: Routledge.

Gladwin, M and Collins, J (2008) Anxieties and Risks, in Collins, J and Foley, P (2008) *Promoting Children's Wellbeing: Policy and Practice.* Bristol: The Policy Press. The Open University.

Goleman, D (2006) *Social Intelligence – The New Science of Human Relationships.* London: Hutchinson.

Gopnik, A, Meltzoff, A and Kuhl, P (2001) *How Babies Think.* London: Phoenix.

Griffin, A and Fein, G (2009) *Infant Day Care: The Critical Issues* www.kidsource.com/kidsource/content2/Infant_Day_Care.html accessed 24 May 2010.

Guerin, D W, Gottfried, A W and Thomas, C W (1997) Difficult Temperament and Behaviour Problems: A Longitudinal Study From 1.5 to 12 Years. *International Journal of Behavioural Development,* 21: 71–90.

Hackman, JR (2002) *Leading Teams.* Harvard: Harvard University Press.

Harter, S (1983) Developmental Perspectives on the Self-system, in Mussen, P H (ed.) *Handbook of Child Psychology,* vol. 4, New York: Wiley.

Hill, G (2009) *Signing with Children* available on The Early Years Foundation Stage Forum available at www.foundation-stage.info/newfsf/articles/visitors/FSFArticle_296.php accessed 24 May 2010.

Johnson, M H (2000) Functional Brain Development in Infants: Elements of an Interactive Specialization Framework, *Child Development,* 71: 75–81.

Johnson, M H and Morton, J (1991) *Biology and Cognitive Development: The Case of Face Recognition.* Oxford: Blackwell.

Karmiloff-Smith, A (1994) *Baby It's You: A Unique Insight into the First Three Years of the Developing Baby.* London: Ebury Press, Random House.

Kohn, M (2009) *Self-Interest and the Common Good.* Oxford: Oxford University Press.

Laevers, F (ed.) (1994) *The Leuven Involvement Scale for Young Children (manual and video) Experiential Education Series, No. 1.* Leuven: Centre for Experiential Education.

Luff, P (2009) Observation for Relational Pedagogy, in Papatheodorou, T and Moyles, J *Learning Together in the Early Years: Exploring Relational Pedagogy.* London: Routledge.

Maccoby, E (1980) *Social Development, Psychological Growth and the Parent–Child Relationship.* New York: Harcourt Brace Jovanovich.

Maccoby, E E and Martin, J A (1983) Socialization in the Context of the Family: Parent–Child Interaction, in Hetherington, E M (ed.) *Mussen Manual of Child Psychology*, Vol. 4, New York: Wiley, pp1–102.

Maclean, P (1990) *The Triune Brain in Evolution.* New York: Plenum Press.

Malaguzzi, L (1993) For an Education Based on Relationships. *Young Children,* 47(1): 9–12.

Manning-Morton, J and Thorp, K (2001) *Key Times: A Framework for Developing High Quality Provision for Children Under Three Years Old.* London Borough of Camden: Camden Early Years Under Threes Development Group.

Mathieson, K (2004) *Social Skills in the Early Years, Supporting Social and Behavioural Learning.* London: Paul Chapman Publishing.

McMullen, M and Dixon, S (2009) A Relationship-Based Approach to Practice with Infants and Toddlers in the United States, in Berthelsen, D, Brownlee, J and Johansson, E (eds.) *Participatory Learning in the Early Years: Research and Pedagogy.* London: Routledge.

McNeil, F (2009) *Learning with the Brain in Mind.* London: Sage.

McTavish, A, (2008) *Creative Solutions to Early Years Behaviour,* Early Years Update, May 2008 www.teachingexpertise.com/articles/creative-solutions-early-years-behaviour-3716 accessed 24 May 2010.

Miell, D (1995) Developing a Sense of Self, in Barnes, P (ed.) *Personal, Social and Emotional Development of Children.* Oxford: Blackwell. The Open University.

Mitchell, J (2009) Riding in Tandem – The Art of Co-regulation, in *Adoption Today,* August 2009, Adoption UK.

Mosley, J (2005a) *Circle Time Handbook.* Trowbridge: Positive Press Ltd.

Mosley, J (2005b) *Circle Time for Young Children.* Nursery World/Routledge.

Mosley, J and Sonnet, H (2005) *Better Behaviour through Golden Time.* Cambridge: LDA.

Moyles, J, Adams, S and Musgrove, A (2002) *SPEEL: Study of Pedagogical Effectiveness in Early Learning.* London: DfES. Report No. 363.

National Children's Bureau (2009) *Listening as a Way of Life. Developing a Listening Culture.* London: NCB.

Nurse, A D (2007) *The New Early Years Professional: Dilemmas and Debates.* London: Routledge.

Nutbrown, C and Clough, P (2006) *Inclusion in the Early Years.* London: Sage.

Nyland, B (2009) The Guiding Principle of Participation: Infant, Toddler Group and the United Nations Convention on the Rights of the Child, in Berthelsen, D, Brownlee, J and Johansson, E (eds.) *Participatory Learning in the Early Years: Research and Pedagogy.* London: Routledge.

Oates, R, Sanders, A, Hey, C, White, J, Wood, V and Yates, E (2009) Making a Little Difference for Early Childhood Studies Students, in Papatheodorou, T and Moyles, J *Learning Together in the Early Years: Exploring Relational Pedagogy.* London: Routledge.

O'Neill, O (2002) *A Question of Trust – The BBC Reith Lectures 2002.* Cambridge: Cambridge University Press.

Papatheodorou, T and Moyles, J (2009) *Learning Together in the Early Years: Exploring Relational Pedagogy.* London: Routledge.

Pascal, C and Bertram, T (1999) *The Effective Early Learning Project: The Quality of Adult Engagement in Early Childhood Settings in the UK.* University College Worcester: Centre for Research in Early Childhood Education.

Payler, J (2009) Co-constructing Meaning. Ways of Supporting Learning, in Papatheodorou, T and Moyles, J *Learning Together in the Early Years: Exploring Relational Pedagogy.* London: Routledge.

Peters, S (2009) Responsive, Reciprocal Relationships: The Heart of the Te Whāriki Curriculum, in Papatheodorou, T and Moyles, J (2009) *Learning Together in the Early Years. Exploring Relational Pedagogy.* London: Routledge.

Piaget, J (1951) *Play Dreams and Imitation in Childhood.* London: Routledge and Kegan Paul.

Pollard, A (ed.) (2005) *Reflective Teaching* (2nd ed.). London: Continuum.

Rawlings, A (1996) *Ways and Means Today.* Kingston: Kingston Friends Workshop Group.

Rawlings, A (2008) *Studying Early Years: A Guide to Work-Based Learning.* Maidenhead: McGraw-Hill Education Open University Press.

Robins, A (ed.) (2006) *Mentoring in the Early Years.* London: Sage.

Robinson, K (2008) *Signing with Babies and Young Children: Signs for Success* available at www.signsforsuccess.co.uk/index.html accessed 24 May 2010.

Rogers, B and McPherson, E (2008) *Behaviour Management with Young Children. Crucial First Steps with Children 3 –7 Years.* London: Sage.

Rogers, C R (1980) *A Way of Being – the Founder of the Human Potential Movement Looks Back on a Distinguished Career.* New York: Houghton Mifflin Company.

Rogers, C R (1995) *On Becoming a Person: A Therapist's View of Psychotherapy.* New York: Houghton Mifflin Company.

Rogoff, B (1990) *Apprenticeship in Thinking: Cognitive Development in Social Context.* Oxford: Oxford University Press.

Rowson, R (2006) *The Framework for Ethical Thinking in the Professions.* London: Jessica Kingsley.

Sanson, A, Hemphill, S A and Smart, D (2004) Temperament and Social Development, in Smith, P K, Hart, C H *Childhood Social Development.* Oxford: Blackwell.

Schaffer, H R (1996) Joint Involvement Episodes as Context for Development, in Daniels, H (ed.) *An Introduction to Vygotsky.* London: Routledge.

Schore, A (2009) *Plenary Final* made available on www.allanschore.com-pdf-APA accessed 12 October 2009.

Seldon, A (2009a) 'We need trust, not more surveillance.' *The Independent* 12 September 2009 www.independent.co.uk/opinion/commentators/anthony-seldon-we-need-trust-not-more-surveillance-1786161.html accessed 4 May 2010.

Seldon, A (2009b) *Trust. How We Lost It and How To Get It Back.* London: Biteback.

Sheppy, S (2009) *Personal, Social and Emotional Development in the Early Years Foundation Stage.* Oxford: Routledge.

Sheridan, M D, Frost, M and Sharma, A (1997) *From Birth to Five Years: Children's Developmental Progress.* London: Routledge.

Sieratzki, J and Woll, B (2005) Cerebral Asymmetry: From Survival Strategies to Social Behaviour. *Behavioral and Brain Sciences, 28:4 , 613–14.*

Siraj-Blatchford, I, Clarke, K and Needham, M (eds.) (2007) *The Team Around the Child: Multiagency Working in the Early Years.* Stoke on Trent: Trentham Books.

Siraj-Blatchford, I, Sylva, K, Muttock, S, Gilden, R and Bell, D (2002) *Researching Effective Pedagogy in the Early Years.* Queen's Publisher. DfES.

Smith, C (1998) Children with Special Rights in the PrePrimary Schools and Infant-Toddler Centers of

Reggio Emilia, in Edwards, C P, Gandini, L and Forman, G (eds.) *The Hundred Languages of Children: The Reggio Emilia Approach – Advanced Reflections.* London: JAI Press.

Smith, P K, Cowie, H and Blades, M (1991) *Understanding Children's Development – Fourth Edition.* Oxford: Blackwell.

Stacey, M (2009) *Teamwork and Collaboration in Early Years Settings.* Exeter: Learning Matters.

Sylva, K and Lunt, I (1982) *Child Development: A First Course.* Oxford: Basil Blackwell.

Thomas, A and Chess, S (1977) *Temperament and Development.* New York: Brunner/Mazel.

Thomas, A and Chess, S (1986) The New York Longitudinal Study: From Infancy to Early Adult Life, in Plomin, R and Dunn, J (eds.) *Changes, Continuities and Challenges.* Hillsdale, NJ: Erlbaum.

Tizard, B and Hughes, M (1984) *Young Children Learning: Talking and Thinking at Home and at School.* London: Fontana.

Trevarthen, C (1993) The Function of Emotions in Early Infant Communication and Development, in Nadel, J and Camaioni, L (eds.) *New Perspectives in Early Communicative Development.* London: Routledge.

Trevarthen, C (2004) *Learning about Ourselves from Children: Why a Growing Human Brain Needs Interesting Companions* www.perception-in-action.ed.ac.uk/PDF_s/colwyn2004.pdf

Trinder, L (2005) *Messages From Research about Children's Needs, Outcomes and Interventions in Separated Families* www.fatherhoodinstitute.org/index.php?id=4&cID=210 accessed 24 May 2010

Turner, R H (1968) The Self-conception in Social Interaction, in Gordon, C and Gergen, K J (eds.) *The Self in Social Interaction,* vol.1, New York: Wiley.

United Nations Convention on the Rights of the Child (1989) www.unicef.org/crc/ accessed 15 February 2010.

Unicef Fact Sheet: A Summary of the Rights Under the Convention on the Rights of the Child www.unicef.org/crc/files/Rights_overview.pdf accessed 15 February 2010.

VOICE www.voicetheunion.org.uk/index.cfm/page/why_voice.cfm/ncid/1055 accessed 6 January 2010.

Vygotsky, L (1978) *Mind in Society.* (Trans. M. Cole). Cambridge, MA: Harvard University Press.

Vygotsky, L (2002) *Language and Thought.* Cambridge, MA: The MIT Press (edited and revised by Alex Kozulin).

Weare, K (2004) *Developing the Emotional Literate School.* London: Paul Chapman.

Wenger, E (1998) *Communities of Practice Learning, Meaning and Identity.* Cambridge: Cambridge University Press.

Whalley, M (2007) *Parents Involved in their Children's Learning (PICL): The Pen Green Framework for Engaging Parents.* Pen Green Research.

Whalley, M E (2008) *Leading Practice in Early Years Settings.* Exeter: Learning Matters.

White, M (2008) *Magic Circles: Self-esteem for Everyone in Circle Time* (2nd ed.). London: Lucky Duck BooksSage.

Wood, D (1998) *How Children Think and Learn* (2nd ed.). Oxford: Blackwell.

Index

abuse 61–4
action-reflection cycle 109
active listening 45, 51; *see also* tuning-in
active reflective learning groups 51
affirmation 28, 29
agency 33
agent of change, EYP as 97
ages and stages approach to child development 80
aggression 56
anger 56
appraisals 96
assertive communication skills 56
assertive strategies 44–5
Association for Teachers and Lecturers (ATL) 52
Association of Professionals in Education and
    Children's Trusts (ASPECT) 52
athletic competence 37
attachment theory (Bowlby) 6–7, 19, 75, 82, 106
'attunement' 12, 92

Baby Peter 65, 66
behavioural control 37
Birth to Three Matters 80, 106, 112
'blame' statements 101
body language 43, 44
Boundaries for the Key Person role 59–61
boundary-setting 45
brain development 12, 17–18, 74–5
bullying 52

Candidates on the Pathway 95
catalysts for change 4
categorical self 35
Child Involvement Scale 90
Childcare Act 2006 32, 53
Children Act: 1989 32; 2004 32, 53
Children's Centres 89, 95, 112
Children's Workforce 112
circle activities 45
circle time 45, 48
clarity of role 109
coaching 108
co-construction 119–20
cognitive intelligence 17
collaborative communication skills 69
'collaborative working' 97
Common Assessment Framework (CAF) 66–8
Common Core of Skills and Knowledge 7, 54, 55,
    56, 58
communication skills 16, 55, 96
communication theories (Vygotsky) 36

Communication, Language and Literacy (CLL) 36, 80
communities of practice 118
confidentiality 109
conflict: appropriate responses to 56; recognition
    of 43–5
congruence 5, 55
CONSPEC (conspecific face recognition system) 15
constructive behaviour 43
constructive humour 45
containment 45
'contingent response' 99
co-operative skills 96
co-regulation 106–7
Creative Development (CD) 37, 80
credibility 109
'cue in' 12, 22, 36
curiosity 20
Curriculum Guidance for the Foundation Stage 80,
    112

developmental stages (Erickson) 76, 85
do's and don'ts 42–3

Early Years Foundation Stage (EYFS) 36, 37, 80
Early Years Professional Status Pathways to
    Validation 82
Early Years Professional Support Networks 118,
    120
'ecological model' of development
    (Bronfenbrenner) 32, 73, 78, 112
Effective Early Learning (EEL) project 90
effective practice 112
emotional abuse 52
emotional empathy 106
emotional intelligence 29, 69
emotional literacy 22, 43, 106
empathic understanding 6, 8, 22, 45, 55, 98, 106
environment, growth/learning 5
'Ethic of Care' 61
ethics within reflective practice 120–1
Every Child Matters (ECM) 7, 10, 53, 64, 72, 112
'exo-system' 32

facial expression 19, 43, 44
facial recognition 15
FAIR model 120
false allegations 52
Fatherhood Institute 103
feelings vocabulary 43, 101
fight/flight/freeze responses 17
First Impressions 12–14

'Fish Day' 116–17, 118
Forest Schools 115

'genuineness' 5, 44, 55, 98, 104–5, 106
'Golden Rules' 43
'growth-promoting climate' 5, 96, 98, 106

'Hello'/'Goodbye' routines 23, 24
'hide and seek'-type activities 24
'Hierarchy of Needs' (Maslow) 29–30
holistic approach 2, 36, 46, 114
holistic learning 18, 52, 112
'How?' questions 20

'imitation' 33
inclusive practice 47
Independent Safeguarding Authority (ISA) 64
infant directed speech (IDS) (motherese) 17
infant school exclusions 56–7
'insecure attachment' 19
internal working model 19
interviews, formal 96
intimacy 21
intuitive thinking 99

key person 6–7, 58–9, 82
Knowledge and Understanding of the World (KUW)
    37, 80

Lead Professional, skills and knowledge 67
learning dispositions 108
'Learning Journeys' 35
levels of relationship 6–7
life-span development, stages of (Erikson) 6
limbic system 17–18
Listening as a Way of Life 55, 120
'listening culture' 52, 55, 61, 99, 104
Listening Cycle, The 56
looking 13
looking-glass self 33
love 59–60

'macro-system' 32
'me' and 'mine', use of 36–7
'mediation' 74
mediator skills 108
meditation 115
men as Key Persons 62–3
mentoring 51, 96, 108–9
'meso-system' 32
'mindful' of the moment 23, 51, 59, 68, 76, 92, 109
'mindful' practice 9, 27, 69, 72, 110, 122
'mirror moments' 4
mirror neurons 23
mirrors, use of 34
'miscues' 19, 21–2
mistrust 6
mother/infant mutual gaze 16

mother-ese/parent-ese dialogue 75
multi-agency working 52
multiple attachments 59, 75, 89, 108
mutual respect 45

'nappy curriculum' 57
National Children's Bureau (NCB): Young Children's
    Voices Network Project 55
National Curriculum Key Stages 79
negative relationships 2
neglect 52
neuroscience 74–5
neutral relationships 2
night and day childcare provision 46
'No', use of 19–20
'no-blame' approach 45
non-verbal communication 18, 51

observation skills 45

parental belief systems 38, 39
parenting styles, classification of (Baumrind) 40
parents as partners 39–40
Parents Involved in their Children's Learning (PICL)
    101–2
'participation' 119
'peek-a-boo' activities 24
Persona Dolls 43
Personal, Social and Emotional Development (PSED)
    36, 80
personality 41–2
physical abuse 52
physical appearance 37
physical closeness and holding 61–4
Physical Development (PD) 37, 80
PILESS (Physical, Intellectual, Language, Emotional,
    Social and Spiritual Development; PIES; PILES)
    79, 80
positive learning dispositions 89–90
positive relationships 1–10; definition 4; EYPs in
    establishing 5–6; leading and supporting others
    95–6
positive strokes 29
positiveness of contact 16
posture 19
'power' elements in relationships 97
praise 37–9
pre-assessment checklist, CAF 66
precautionary principle 61
primary attachment 2, 8, 15, 19, 59, 75, 89
Principles into Practice cards 97, 107; Respecting
    each other (2.1) 100–2; Parents as Partners (2.2)
    102–4; Supporting Learning (2.3) 104–5; Key
    Person (2.4) 105–9
Problem-Solving, Reasoning and Numeracy (PSRN)
    37, 80
professional boundaries: to respect children 53–4;
    with parents/other professionals 64–5

professional intimacy, appropriate 61
professionalism in reflection and learning 114–15
'proto-conversations' 12, 17
provision, prevention, promotion and participation programmes 79

quality improvement 97

realness 5, 55
reflection 9, 45, 68, 122
reflective learning community 118–20
reflective learning cycle 117–18
reflective listening 101–2
'reflective' practice 6, 9, 27, 69, 72, 110, 113, 115–16, 121, 122
reflective practitioners 112–13
Reggio Emilia approach 73, 115, 118
'reification' 119
'relational pedagogy' 54, 74–80, 89, 92, 98
relationship-based approach 4, 23, 46, 69, 72, 92
relationship development 80–91
relationship skills, leader characteristics 97–108
Researching Effective Pedagogy in the Early Years (REPEY) 73, 74
resilience 3, 22, 85
respect 48, 68; for colleagues 28; definition 27–6; for others 42–7; by separating 'behaviour' from the child 42–3
'respectful' practice 9, 27, 30, 44, 69, 72, 109, 110, 122
Responsiveness Cordial 22, 51, 61, 75
risk-taking 3
role-modelling 108, 109
'rupture and repair' 106,107

Safeguarding Vulnerable Groups Act (2006) 64
'scaffolding' 74, 76–7
schemas 76
scholastic competence 37
secondary attachment 12, 59, 75
secondary relationships 107
'secure attachment' 19
self-awareness 38, 113
self-esteem 35–6, 38, 48
self-identity 30–5, 48, 56
'self-image' 28
self-motivation 113
self-respect 30–5, 42–7
self-worth 35–6
sensitive responsiveness 18, 24
sexual abuse 52
shared histories of learning 119
signing with babies and young children 47
similarities, looking for 15
smell 13, 14
smile 15
social acceptance 37
social and emotional literacy 24

social constructivist theories 53, 78
social learning theories (Bandura) 36
social referencing 16, 23
'sorry' 45
spiritual self 115
staff appraisals 108
staff conflict 44
staff induction 108
storytelling 48
Study of Pedagogical Effectiveness in Early Learning (SPEEL) 73, 74
supervision sessions 51
support: Key Person approach with 0–20 month olds 83; relationships 45–6
Sure Start Research Reports: *Use of Childcare Among Families with Children who have Special Educational Needs* 103; *Use of Childcare Among Families from Minority Ethnic Backgrounds* 103
Sustained, shared thinking 90, 91
synergy 72

Tavistock Method of Observation 106
'Te Whariki' 58, 73, 89, 115
temper tantrums 85
temperament 41–2
three Ps (provision; protection; participation) 53, 54
time management for support and leadership 98
touch 13, 14, 62
traffic lights approach to emotional states 107
'Tri-une Brain' (Maclean) 17
trust 109; abuse of position of 63–4; definition 3–4; national picture 7–8; reason for 1–10
tuning-in 2, 3, 13, 16, 17–21, 24, 44, 45
tuning-out 12, 16, 23–4

unconditional love 18, 24
'unconditional positive regard' 5, 55, 98, 106
unconscious responses 18
United Nations Convention on the Rights of the Child (UNCRC) 53

validation, EYP 78–9, 80
Validation Pathways 85
verbal communication 18, 51
Vetting and Barring Scheme (2010) 64
violence 56
VOICE 52
voice, tone of 19

'whole-setting approach' 97
'Why?' questions 20

Young Children's Voices Network 56, 120

'Zone of Proximal Development' (ZPD) 74, 76